To Frank & Mrs. Pearce. With many thanks for
all the years you've put up with me! Hope
you enjoy this.

The Polish Exile

Michael Oakeshott

1.5.93

The Polish Exile

Michael Pakenham

The Pentland Press Limited
Edinburgh · Cambridge · Durham

By the same author:
The Bitter Web

First published in 1993 by
The Pentland Press Ltd.
1 Hutton Close
South Church
Bishop Auckland
Durham

ISBN 1 85821 041 0

Typeset by Elite Typesetting Techniques, Southampton.
Printed and bound by Antony Rowe Ltd., Chippenham.

To Dermot, Caroline & Rebecca
with all my love

Author's Note

I drove my well-worn route to the Chestnut Horse at Easton, just a few miles outside Winchester, to meet John Mieszkowski for lunch. For many months it had been our meeting place to discuss *The Polish Exile* and for me to give him another few pages to read. Over a glass of wine, he had recounted endless stories of his father, Albert Mieszkowski, and corrected me on historical facts. Today, however, was going to be different, and I felt a lump in my throat as I entered the bar and saw him as usual standing talking to the landlord, immaculately dressed as I imagined his father always to have been. For this was to be our last meeting and the end of an absorbing journey for me. My task was almost complete and I held in my hand the last part of *The Polish Exile*.

As usual we ordered our drinks and then moved to the little table by the window where we had sat every time we had met. It was almost exactly a year since I had written the first word of *The Polish Exile*, but a few months longer since John had introduced me to the fascinating story of his family and Poland, and I had started my research. I feel I know the Mieszkowskis well, and I have certainly learnt a lot about their country, its brave people and their fight against the Nazis and their years of living under Communism. Not to mention brave men like Andre Zaluski, Paul Jankowski and the many others that played, at different times, such important roles in Albert Mieszkowski's life.

I had almost felt his pain as he lost these friends and comrades, and I would dearly have loved to have met Helene Milosevo who I suspect, in spite of Alicia Pachalska, was his one great love, although there is nothing to contradict his assertion that he would never have married her.

It is particularly fitting, I feel, that while I was writing *The Polish Exile*, Eastern Europe should so suddenly and dramatically throw off Communism and that at last Poland has become a free country, facing I fear many problems yet. But I'm sure they are well capable of mastering them in the end. As a nation they have had a mixed and sometimes violent past, and they need the West's support which, I think it fair to say, has sometimes been sadly lacking. Now that Communism has been cast off the chance is there, for Britain at least, to make amends for her pathetic response to Poland's cries for help in the past.

Stalin once said that trying to establish Communism in Poland was like trying to fit a saddle on a cow. Successive Communist leaders I feel would agree with him, and now the people have a chance to enter the new world of capitalism.

Having finished our drinks I handed over the last part of the book for John to read. It was a funny feeling, realising that I would not be going home to sit in front of the word processor or to read a page of Albert's diary. I had all but finished – a void in my life would soon need filling.

It was raining as we made our way back to our cars, and as I watched the Discovery pull away I felt a little sad that John would never live at Mieszki Wielkie. I felt the old house was probably still waiting for a Mieszkowski to return.

For me it had certainly been an interesting year, and of one thing I'm certain, I will never forget Albert Mieszkowski, the suffering of his countrymen, or their unremitting drive for freedom.

In the preparation of this book I would like to thank John Mieszkowski for his unstinting support, who, apart from our Chestnut Horse meetings, has put up with incessant telephone calls; his wife Vicky who, with great cheerfulness, seemed to track John down in places as far apart as Hamburg and the Spey in Scotland; Fiona my wife, for endlessly sorting me out on the word processor, whenever it was in one of its bloody-minded moods.

On historical facts, dates and events, I have received considerable help from Martin Gilbert's book *The Second World War*; Adam Zamoyski's *The Polish Way*; Irena and Jerzy Kostrowicki's *Poland*; The Interpress Publisher's *A Panorama of Polish History*; and the Cambridge *History of Poland Part One*. And finally I must thank all the other people who have given me invaluable information about the war, Hungary, and life in France under the German occupation.

I hope the end result is a fitting tribute to all those men and women whose bravery between 1939 and 1945 has gone unrecorded, and therefore never had the recognition they deserve, from what should be an extremely grateful world.

Preface

On 1 September 1939 some 1.8 million German troops invaded Poland. On 3 September France and Great Britain declared war on Hitler and then did little to come to Poland's aid. Her army was hopelessly outnumbered and when the Russians invaded from the east on 17 September even the most optimistic Pole had to admit that defeat could not be long in coming. An assumption that soon proved correct, for on 5 October, in the small town of Koch, east of Warsaw, General Keeber surrendered to the Germans, and the remnants of the Polish army either went underground, or made their way to France and England so that they could fight another day. In spite of the persecution, torture, and almost certain death if they were caught, the people of Poland went on fighting the Germans – their spirit never broken.

The Poles were possibly the nation that suffered most in the Second World War. They never stopped fighting and they put more effort into their struggle than any other society. The horrifying statistics speak for themselves. They lost over half a million fighting men and women and six million civilians. They were left with one million war orphans and over half a million invalids. The country lost 38% of its national assets, lost vast tracts of country and, although they were part of the victorious alliance, they were treated more like a vanquished army – robbed of much of their territory and their freedom.

This is the story of Albert Mieszkowski, one of the many unsung heroes of the Second World War, and his life after hostilities had ended. He was one of Poland's aristocratic élite, bred to inherit the power and privileges of his father and a large estate in the east of Poland, and to live a comfortable life surrounded by servants and land on which to enjoy himself. Because of man's cruelty to man and the ever-presence of greed, he was never able to take up that inheritance.

ix

He accepted the change with the assurance of a man double his age, and refused to believe that one day his beloved Poland would not once again rise from the ashes of tyranny.

That it has, is in no small way due to men like Albert Mieszkowski, who first of all refused to lie down under the Nazi boot, and then fought on with great spirit and untold bravery to defeat the forces of communism. Many have not lived to see that day, and others suffered terrible degradation and torture, so that their children and grand-children could hopefully live in a free and democratic Poland.

Even in times of great stress, love can still play an important role on the switchback of life, and this story not only tells of human sacrifice and unselfishness, but also illustrates that even in war and times of hardship, there can still be a place for that one great and most exciting emotion.

BALTIC SEA
LATVIA
LITHUANIA
GERMANY
Gdynia
Danzig
EAST
PRUSSIA
Kaunas
Wilno
Bydgoszcz
Grodno
Minsk
Toruń
Nowogródek
Poznań
Białystok
SOVIET
WARSAW
Łódź
Brześć
Pińsk
RUSSIA
Radom
Lublin
Kielce
Łuck
Katowice
Kraków
Kiev
Cieszyn
Lwów
CZECHOSLOVAKIA
RUMANIA

Frontier of Poland in 1772 ——
Poland 1921–1939
Free city of Danzig

Miles   200
0
km   200

Poland 1921–1939

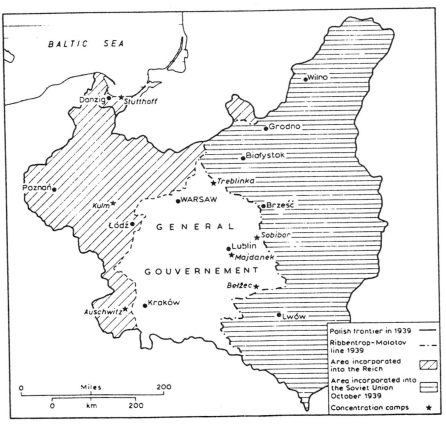

Key:
- Polish frontier in 1939 ———
- Ribbentrop-Molotov line 1939 — · —
- Area incorporated into the Reich
- Area incorporated into the Soviet Union October 1939
- Concentration camps ★

The Nazi-Soviet partition of Poland, 1939

PART ONE

APRIL 1938 – SEPTEMBER 1939

Chapter 1

Mieszki Wielkie was a typical estate of the landed aristocracy of Poland, occupying some 20,000 hectares in the east of the country around the town of Lvov. It encompassed six villages and gave a livelihood to hundreds of peasants. The house, which sat in the middle of the estate, had been built by the first Mieszkowski in the seventeenth century and generations of the family had survived the ebb and flow of Polish history including many years of partition by Russia.

On the last day of April 1938 Albert Mieszkowski came out of the woods with his sister Barbara and looked up at the large grey stone house gazing benevolently down at them, its dozens of windows glistening in the rays of the afternoon spring sun.

He turned to smile at her. 'I always feel happy when I come back here – there is something so peaceful about the place – as if it was in another world where unhappiness does not exist and where time has stood still. It amazes me what a spell Mieszki Wielkie spins over me.'

Barbara squeezed his hand. Something was worrying him. She could sense an inner turmoil but knew from past experience that if he wanted to confide in her he would do it in his own good time.

She would be seventeen in June, and finished with school at last. The younger by six years – an afterthought of her parents – she had always been very close to her brother and loved him deeply. She could still remember the pain that tore at her heart the day he kissed her goodbye as he set out for the Cavalry school in Kracow. She had been sure she would never see him again. The only other time she had felt anything like such pain was on her first night at the convent school where her parents had insisted on sending her. She had never quite forgiven them for that, and she had missed her brother ever since.

3

For no sooner had he completed his cavalry officer's course than he had decided to enter the diplomatic service. She was envious that he could go away and do so many interesting things while she was still a schoolgirl expected to conform to the rigorous discipline of a convent. It had made her a restless and slightly rebellious young lady determined to break away from convention just as soon as she had the chance. It was not that she didn't love her parents or Mieszki Wielkie – it was just that she would have liked to have moved the clock forward so that she could be as adventurous as her brother. Her parents understood her restlessness and smiled sympathetically. 'Your turn will come,' was their customary answer whenever she voiced her impatience.

In spite of their long separations, the bond between brother and sister had, if anything, grown stronger, and the surge of excitement she felt whenever he came home never weakened.

This time he was back for a month, and luckily it coincided with her holidays. It was his second visit since becoming third secretary in the Paris Embassy, and already nearly two weeks had gone by and she had not found a moment to be on her own with him. He had seemed preoccupied and withdrawn – not normally his nature at all.

Then at last they had gone on a walk alone, but she had been forced to bite her tongue all the way along the forest tracks as, much to her dismay, he had shuffled dejectedly in front of her, kicking at the dead leaves and hitting out at the odd tree with his walking stick without saying a word.

Now as they stood in the sunshine his silence had been broken . . .

'I really don't want to lose this place, you know. I miss it more than ever now that I'm away so much.'

Barbara looked up into his eyes. 'I understand that – but why on earth should you lose it?'

He shrugged. 'I just have a feeling, although there is no reason why it should concern you.'

'I'm not stupid, you know,' she said angrily. 'Even in the convent we hear things and I know all about the German danger. Please tell me why you have this fear?'

'I'm sorry, I didn't mean to treat you like a child. It is just that I don't want to upset you. But if you insist . . .'

'I do.'

Albert shrugged. 'Very well. You see, there are many disturbing rumours doing the rounds in Paris at the moment. No doubt they abound in Poland as well. It's after this Austrian business. Hitler is rumoured to have designs on us and he is a cunning bastard. Quite a few people in the know think that if he attacked us now our allies would not come to our aid.'

'Surely France and England won't let us down? We are continually being told at school that they are our friends.'

'Ha! The talk in the diplomatic service is that neither of them will lift a finger to help us, and I fear that could be right. To be honest, I can't see that we have any dependable allies, reserves of power or crucial facilities. We are simply not worth going to war for.'

'Don't we have a non-aggression pact with Germany?'

'Yes. However, as I have just said, informed opinion is that we can't trust Hitler. And I'm sure that if he invades us, Russia won't be far behind and then everything round here could be engulfed by hoards of Bolsheviks.'

'Oh Albert, shut up! I simply refuse to believe your depressing predictions! Mieszki Wielkie will always be ours!'

He gave her a weak smile. 'You be optimistic, darling sister, if you like, but whatever happens in the next few years, I can see the old order changing.' He swung his hand around in an arc. 'Have we the right as a family to own all this? We still have vast tracts of land in spite of the land reform. And has that done the peasants any good? By God, no! They have too few hectares to generate enough income. I thought it was a good idea, but it simply hasn't worked. Look at us – still rich and powerful. Father still has vast wealth and many servants – enjoys himself whenever the mood takes him and extracts rent from people who can only just afford to feed themselves, to pay for all his amusements! It has to change, you know. Take Russia, I honestly believe they have set the trend.'

Barbara tightened her grip on his hand. 'I hope father doesn't hear you say that! Since when have you developed such a radical conscience? Surely it is not life in Paris?'

He laughed. 'No, no, far from it. Only a few share my views –but I think I'm a realist and they are blinkered. I have seen and heard things on my travels that have convinced me that sooner or later things are going to change in this part of Europe. I honestly believe that we cannot justify our enormous wealth when so many of our countrymen are nearly starving. How can I expect you to understand that, shut away in a convent or listening to our parents? Everyone here lives in the past.'

Barbara was silent for a moment. 'I can't bring myself to believe you,' she finally said. 'Besides, you have used your privileged position without too much complaining, I have noticed.'

He looked down at her and ruffled her long dark hair. He loved her so much. He saw the uncertainty written on her face. Somehow it accentuated her prettiness. She had always reminded him of a Dresden doll – finely made and easily broken, and when she had been a little girl, he had felt he could see vulnerability mirrored in her blue eyes. She had not changed.

'I know, I know. And I have loved every minute of my life so far, especially here. I just fear a chapter is about to end. Actually, in many ways I envy you – your ideal dream is still intact. I have changed. I see things differently to you now, and that has made me feel guilty. You know me – I have always spoken my mind. I'm sure you wouldn't want it any other way. We have never hidden our thoughts from each other, have we?'

She looked at him sadly – Oh God, he had grown up so! 'Of course not. But sometimes you are so direct, and what you say frightens me.'

She brushed his lips lightly with her fingers. He was just over six foot – five inches taller than her. He looked so serious –the twinkle in his clear brown eyes that she loved so much was missing, and his wide friendly mouth was without its usual smile. There was a worried look on his face and she thought he was even slimmer than on his last visit. He was still very handsome, and she had no doubt that the young girls of Paris sought his company as much as the aristocratic beauties had done when they had come to stay at Mieszki Wielkie.

He held her hand to his face. 'It is good that you are frightened. You must be on your guard from now on. For everyone like us is in grave danger – Hitler holds no more love for the Polish aristocracy than he does for the Jews.'

Barbara's eyes widened. 'You really mean that? He hates us as much as the Jews?'

'I'm afraid so. And if his troops ever look like reaching this part of Poland you must leave before that happens. There will be no time to waste – probably no time to take much of our heritage, for I know father will be determined to hang on here until the last minute. So unless I can succeed in persuading him to move some things now, I doubt if he will be able to save very much if and when the time comes to flee.'

'Now you really are frightening me. Leave all this just like that?' She snapped her fingers. 'Our home, our possessions, our friends and all the people who depend on us?'

'That's what I'm saying. Surely you would rather still have your life? None of this is any good to you if you are dead.'

'But where would we go?'

'To England. We have friends there already.'

'Dear God, Albert! Have you warned father?'

'Yes, and mother. It has taken me nearly two weeks to decide what to say, and it wasn't until this morning that I plucked up enough courage. That is why they were so quiet at lunch. They made me promise to tell you this afternoon – I don't think they wanted to.'

Barbara shook her head. 'How did they react?'

'Outwardly, remarkably calmly, although I'm sure they are bleeding internally. I don't think father was too surprised. After all, he keeps his ears to the ground.'

'It will break their hearts to leave here.'

'Not quite, I'm sure. They are both realists and I think accept that if either the Germans or the Russians invade Poland, their position here would be untenable. Of course, it is no use pretending that it won't be a wrench. My God, who would want to leave all this behind.' He paused for a second and looked at his sister's crestfallen face. 'Of course, there is always the chance that I'm being too pessimistic, but I have a gut feeling I'm right.'

'I hope to God you aren't.'

She looked round her. Mieszki Wielkie in the spring was beautiful. It was her favourite time. Perhaps it was something to do with the disappearance of the winter snow and the freshness of all the colours around her. It was the time when she felt she belonged to a heritage worth keeping – and yet here was her brother telling her that it was all about to end. She would miss the old house – the mountains and the lakes – there could be no more magical place on earth. She angrily brushed away a tear and looked at their father's Hispano Suiza parked by the front door and the deep blue sky above the slated roof of the house. It was difficult in this perfect setting to believe that anything could go wrong.

She shivered. 'You have said enough. Come on, let's go inside. You have made me thoroughly depressed.'

They walked hand in hand across the drive and into the house. The vast hall, its walls lined with family portraits, echoed to their footsteps as they walked across the stone floor to the drawing room where Albert was sure they would find their parents discussing his disturbing news. He hesitated momentarily at the closed door. 'Do you know, I hate myself right now. Perhaps I should have said nothing.'

Barbara shook her head. 'No, no. You were right to warn us. If any of us choose not to believe you, that is our problem.'

'Do you believe me?'

'Yes, I think I do. I know you are not the sort of person to panic easily or to act on a whim. You have seldom spoken anything else but sense.'

'Thank God for that. I hope father is the same. Mother? Well, I have never been able to fathom what she is thinking.'

Barbara laughed. 'I think that has always been her idea, hasn't it? Don't you remember how she used to keep us guessing when we were children? It was one of her favourite games. She is still playing it – not only with us, but with father as well. I think he rather enjoys it.'

'Yes, I suppose so, but it is damned annoying sometimes. Like today, for instance. It would be much better for her if she shared her thoughts with us. Locking them away only makes them seem worse.'

The voice of Jacek Mieszkowski came through the door. 'Stop whispering, you two out there, and come on in.'

Barbara laughed as she pushed the door open. 'Your ears always were too sharp, father!' she said, running over to the armchair where he was sitting and kissing him fondly on the cheek, before moving to sit on the floor beside her mother.

Krystina Mieszkowski squeezed her wet handkerchief into a ball and gave her daughter a watery smile. 'Hello, darling – has your brother been filling you full of his dreadful ideas?'

Barbara looked up at her and nodded.

Fear was written all over her mother's features and Barbara winced with pain. What an age to have to face the possible ruin of such an idyllic life. At seventeen she would be able to adjust, but it would not be so easy for her parents, in their fifties. Especially having to live the life of refugees far from their home, and robbed of all the creature comforts that they had taken for granted for so many years.

'Oh mother, I am so sorry.'

'Don't be, child. I'm just being stupid. The trouble is, your father and I have grown used to luxury. Perhaps a little hardship in middle age will do us no harm. But, oh my God! Losing all this!' She choked, and cupped Barbara's cheeks in her hands. 'Pray with me that it will never happen!'

It was then that Barbara felt her father's hand on her shoulder and she reached up to stroke it, never taking her eyes off her mother. She had not quite inherited her beauty for she had her father's rather large nose, but she had the same delicate skin and fine bone features. Even at fifty, her mother had kept her beauty and when she smiled her entire face softened. Her skin was still smooth to the touch and there was hardly a wrinkle to be seen. Years of pampered attention made her look at least ten years younger.

Jacek coughed. 'Enough of this sadness, Krystina. It will get us nowhere.' He patted Barbara's shoulder. 'Why don't you take your mother out into the garden – Albert and I have some things to discuss.'

'Meaning that they are not for our ears?' asked Barbara.

He spoke firmly, broaching no objection. 'Precisely, and anyway they will bore you; and besides, your mother needs some fresh air.'

Barbara smiled. Sometimes he still treated her as if she was a child. A year ago it had annoyed her, now it rather amused her.

'Oh, very well. Come on, mother – the boys have things to talk about.'

She stood up. 'A walk will do us good anyway. It will clear away the depression.'

'I suppose you are right, darling. It's no good spending every hour from now on waiting in fear of the Germans or the Russians. We will just have to get on with our lives until Albert's disaster arrives.'

As they drew level with Albert, his mother stopped. 'I know what you are thinking, young man. It is written all over your face. Don't feel like that – you had to tell us of your fears. I pray to God they are wrong, but you were right to warn us.'

Krystina touched his arm. 'I just can't imagine ever leaving all this.'

Without waiting for a reply, she turned quickly and pulled Barbara out of the room.

No sooner had the door shut than Jacek lowered himself back into his armchair and looked up at his son.

'Now tell me – how long do you think we've got?'

'It is hard to say, father. In Paris we keep hearing that Hitler intends to invade the Sudetenland.'

Jacek sat bolt upright. 'No!'

'Well, that is what our intelligence people report. Another thing – but please do not repeat this to anyone – it is being said that if he does, we will reoccupy the Zaolzie to protect our southern flank against his army.'

'God, that would be sheer folly! Can you imagine what the liberals in Britain and France would say? "There go those war-mongering Poles again. No better than the Germans or the Italians. Why should we go to war for them?"'

'Is that what you think, father?'

'Well, just look at our history. Unfortunately we have a reputation for being bullies in some very important circles abroad. We would be playing into those people's hands. No, our best chance is to sit quietly, and let Hitler invade us if that is what he intends to do. Then the English and French might feel sorry for us.'

Albert gave a bitter laugh. 'If you believe that, father, you are a bigger fool than I thought you were. Anyway, I suspect it will be the Russians that we will have to keep our eyes on. Do you think they will let Germany occupy this part of eastern Poland? I doubt it. After all, we have been part of Russia this century. However, it is of no matter. The Russians will be as bad as the Germans now that the Tsar has gone, so either way, whoever invades us, it spells trouble for us.'

'You paint a terrible picture, Albert.'

Albert looked at his father's tall frame hunched up in the armchair. It seemed he had aged by years since their talk a few hours before, and all colour had drained from his cheeks. He was not used to seeing him like this – in fact, he couldn't recall a time when he had seen him look so shattered. It was alien to his nature. Normally an outward going man, with his brown eyes flashing mischievously beneath large bushy eyebrows, he had seemed to his children indefatigable, and his fairness was greatly admired by those who worked on the Estate and respected by his family and friends. From an early age Albert had acknowledged that he would be a hard man to follow.

Jacek rubbed his large nose. 'I wonder what will happen to this place and all the priceless things in the house if we are forced to leave? I have a feeling that once we are gone we will never return.'

'I don't know the answers any more than you do, father. So why not pack some of the more valuable things away now? You could at least get them to Paris.'

Jacek shook his head firmly. 'No, no, that would be defeatist and alarm the whole estate. Better to go on as if we fear nothing and be content to take as many of the small valuables as we can if we are forced to leave.'

Albert knew it was no good arguing. 'It was only a suggestion.'

'I know. But to tell you the truth, I'm not sure I will care. I don't expect you to understand, but right now I feel that if I have to leave I would rather turn my back on it all – no reminders of a life I will have to forget. Amputate it, Albert, and start again.' He looked up into the worried face of his son. 'Leave me now, will you? I need a little time to think and compose myself before your mother returns – it is her happiness that must be in all our minds now.'

Albert smiled. It was typical of his father to think of others. 'Very well, I will go and try and find the women. Are you sure you will be all right?'

'All right!' laughed Jacek. 'You know me – I'm always all right!'

Albert smiled again. 'See you later, then.'

He walked out of the room reluctantly. He would have liked to have stayed and talked with his father – there was so much he wanted to say – but perhaps it was not the time. Better to leave him with his thoughts, and wait for a more opportune moment.

He stopped briefly, still wondering what to do. Years later he wrote in his diary: *'I decided not to join mother and Barbara immediately, as I felt I needed a little time on my own. So I looked up at the pictures of my ancestors, hanging on the walls and wondered if they would soon be torn down and tucked away in some German's collection, destroyed by a pillaging mob of filthy Bolsheviks, or hang there for another few generations. The thought filled me with sadness and I decided that I needed to look again at all the treasures packed into the house. I remember going up the stairs and moving from room to room almost as if I was in a dream. I had almost forgotten there were so many. It took much longer than I expected, and every one of them held a different memory for me. The nursery where I had played so many games with Barbara and my parents, the bedroom where I had slept until I was fourteen. My new, much larger, room that I had been so proud of – it had been father's at the same age, and I had felt as if I was inheriting part of the great house. Oh God, there were so many memories! Everywhere there were priceless pictures and furniture – the result of hundreds of years collecting by various Mieszkowskis. As I wandered along the passages and through the rooms I realised how much it would mean to me to lose this inheritance, and if it upset me, what on earth would it do to my father, having to leave all the trappings of centuries of Mieszkowskis behind? Like the house, they had somehow survived the turmoil of Polish history – it seemed almost impossible that their reign might be coming to an end.*

'Nevertheless, cultures were changing fast and the world was becoming more violent and greedy by the day, and I had to admit to myself, as I moved out into the rose garden to find Barbara and mother, that the odds were heavily stacked against me inheriting Mieszki Wielkie and the treasures of the Mieszkowskis.'

Shielding his eyes from the sinking sun he walked past the immaculately kept garden, and passed through a cut yew hedge and on towards the lily pond where he felt his sister and mother might be sitting. It was a quiet spot often frequented by his mother when she had needed a little peace from the bedlam of the house and a demanding family, and sure enough they were sitting on one of the ornate metal benches looking out at the pond. As he approached Albert could see the goldfish rising on the water.

His sister was the first to hear his footsteps. She turned and smiled. 'Finished your private talk, then? It took you long enough.'

His mother pointed to the bench. 'Come and sit down, Albert, and tell us how your father is taking this. He always wants to protect me as if I were some rare flower that will wither up if I get too much exposure. That is just not true – sometimes I think I'm more resilient than he is. I do hope he is not going to shut me out from the pain I know he is suffering. Poor darling, he loves this place so very much. You must talk to him, Albert – tell him to confide in me so that I can share his agony.'

'I will try, mother.'

Albert wrote: *'I remember sitting down and telling them where I had been. Walking round the house, realising what I would be missing if we lost it. Mother became almost hysterical and I had to apologise for being so insensitive.'*

'I understand,' she said sadly. 'It is just difficult to hear you talk like that about the home that one day should be yours. And to think that you won't even be here to help us if your warnings come true. Can you not stay?'

'I wish I could, but I'm needed in Paris and besides, nothing may happen for ages. Come on, let's look on the bright side. I may well be back for Christmas.'

Krystina stood up. 'You were never a good liar and you haven't changed.' She shivered. 'I don't know whether it is getting cold or if it is fear, but I think it is time we went inside.' She linked arms with Albert. 'Come on, young man, give me the pleasure of beating you at chess.'

'One day I will win, mother, I promise,' laughed Albert.

Through one of the drawing room windows, Jacek watched the three people most dear to him walking back to the house. He grimaced and hurried towards the door. Suddenly he didn't want to be alone any more. His family might soon be all he had left.

Two weeks later, Jacek drew the Hispano-Suiza to a halt outside the railway station in Lvov. Sitting beside him, Albert fidgeted nervously. For the first time in his life he didn't feel the excitement that the sight of the station usually engendered in him. The reason was the two empty seats behind him, both Barbara and his mother having decided not to come and see him off.

'We will only make fools of ourselves in front of a lot of people,' Barbara had said when he had asked why. He had looked questioningly at his mother and she had merely nodded. The black rings under her eyes spoke volumes about the distress she was suffering. He had not questioned their decision, but it had not eased the pain of the farewell, and he had left his mother in tears by the front door.

'Come on, hurry up, Albert, or you will miss the train.'

His father's voice made him jump, and he shook his head to try and rid himself of his misery.

He looked at his father as he came round the car. 'Sorry, I was not paying attention.'

He grabbed his one small bag from the back of the car and joined him on the pavement.

'Understandable,' mumbled his father. 'Got your ticket, I hope?'

As they walked hurriedly towards the station entrance, Albert felt in his coat pocket. 'Yes, yes. Please don't feel you have to see me off.'

'Of course I will. Nothing would stop me.' His father smiled and touched his arm.

Albert threw him a grateful look as they joined the jostling and noisy crowd gathered at the entrance to the station. As they pushed and elbowed their way through the crowd, Jacek saw that the train was already getting up steam.

'Quickly now!' he shouted. 'We haven't much time and the last thing you want to do is to have to go back home, eh?'

'My God, you are right there!' gulped Albert, as he ran along beside him. 'I couldn't take another dose of that.'

'Well, come on then!' his father shouted, running onto the platform and grabbing the nearest door. 'Get in, for heaven's sake!'

Albert jumped onto the step, put his case down on the floor and turned to slam the door. He panicked as he saw his father's face through the window – he hadn't said his goodbyes. 'Oh Christ!' He fumbled with the catch and pushed the door open. He was breathing heavily. 'Father, father!'

Jacek took hold of the door. 'Don't worry. I'm not going to run off, and we have a few moments yet, I'm sure.' He playfully punched Albert in the stomach. 'Good luck, young man. Continue to enjoy Paris while you can, and don't worry about us. We will be all right.'

A whistle blew somewhere up the platform. The two men were unashamedly crying and Albert realised it was the first time he had ever seen his father in tears.

'Good luck to you as well, father. You may need it more than me. Remember, make for Paris and the Embassy if you have to. God willing, I will be waiting there for you.'

Another, more urgent, blast of the whistle. 'I must shut the door!' Oh God, parting was painful this time. 'Wait there, I will open the window,' he choked.

By the time he had got the window open the train was moving slowly. 'Goodbye!' Albert shouted, wiping away a tear, 'See you again very soon.'

His father raised a hand. 'Yes, yes, of course you will!'

He ran beside the train until the speed was too great for him to keep up.

He stopped and shouted breathlessly. 'Don't worry, please – everything will work out!'

Albert half raised a hand and remained leaning out of the window until his father disappeared from view. Only then did he push up the window and turn to walk down the corridor in search of his compartment.

He was not used to this feeling of disquiet at leaving home. A little sadness, yes, but there had always been the great excitement of a new challenge to counteract this – another phase of his life about to begin. This time there was no such emotion, his youthful enthusiasm dampened by the black clouds he was sure were gathering above his home. The one question that kept hammering at his brain was: 'Will I ever see my family again?'

He walked along the corridor in a daze, and almost missed his compartment. As was his usual practice on the long journey to Vienna, he had reserved one solely for himself. Today he was even more delighted than usual not to have any fellow passengers interrupting his thoughts.

He pushed back the door and, throwing his case down on one of the seats, pulled the door closed behind him and sat down in the seat nearest the window. Wiping away the tears with his handkerchief he looked out on the countryside racing by. It was one of those marvellous May days that made everything seem just that much more beautiful, and with luck the sun would be out as they wound their way through the Carpathians. The mountain backdrop and the varied hues of the trees intermingling with the snow, and the dark, almost sinister, colour of the deep lakes would be breathtaking at this time of the year. The first leg to Vienna had grown to be his favourite, although he found the whole four-day journey absorbing, but as he tried to make himself comfortable, he realised that this time it was going to drag dreadfully. He kicked irritably at the seat opposite, and wiped away the condensation on the window and found himself staring at his reflection. It could have been his father!

He shook his head angrily – his mind was playing tricks. And yet the vision would not go away. It was too bloody stupid. Annoyed with himself, he pulled back and hastily moved to the other side of the compartment. His hands were shaking so badly that he had to grip his knees to steady them. Perhaps if he closed his eyes . . . Damn! Now he could see Mieszke Wielkie. He let out a cry of despair and reached for his bag. Two days earlier he had bought a black leather-covered diary. Not too big, as he wanted to carry it with him wherever he went. He wondered why he had never kept one before. He blew his nose vigorously and began to write.

Chapter 2

Paris, that May of 1938, was growing pleasantly warm and the cafés were full of Parisiennes shrugging off the bad news of imminent war in the only way they knew how, but there was a touch of urgency in their caresses.

Into this atmosphere Albert returned, a very dejected young man, for, as he had feared, the journey had seemed interminable. Sleep had been almost impossible and he had found his stay in Vienna, waiting for the connecting train, thoroughly disturbing. Arrogant strutting soldiers had been everywhere, creating an aura of disquiet and fear. The atmosphere since his last visit had deteriorated dramatically, and not until he'd had more time to think about it did he realise that it was caused by the unease running through the Jewish population who lived and worked in the city.

Soon however the frenetic mood that pervaded Paris infected him and provided him with something else to think about other than his distant home and family, although they were never far from his thoughts. In one respect he was very lucky: *'For on the staff is one of my greatest friends, Andre Zaluski. It certainly makes life here a good deal more bearable.'*

They had become close friends at the Cavalry School at Kracow and had both decided to join the diplomatic service after their training had finished. They had been inseparable ever since, united by the bond of similar backgrounds. Andre, whose family owned a large estate at Ostrow, west of Warsaw, was much the same build and height as Albert and, with the same coloured eyes, short dark hair and rather large nose, could, at first glance, easily have been mistaken for his twin.

They shared a small flat in the Rue Talleyrand close to the Embassy, and had at first been content to live a quiet life, choosing to spend any evenings they had free at home listening to records and eating meals cooked by Andre. But on Albert's return from Poland their lifestyle

15

changed. No longer were they content to spend these evenings solely in each other's company, tending instead to drift round the cafés, drinking and carousing with the unlimited supply of girls who were hell-bent on having a good time. *'They are brief and enjoyable interludes,'* wrote Albert, *'which end abruptly every morning as we cross the Embassy threshold and are reminded of how tenuous the aura of normality really is.'*

For the news coming into the Embassy was ominous and it left Albert and Andre facing the fact that unless a miracle occurred they would soon be catapulted into the greatest upheaval they had ever experienced in their young lives, and as the days and weeks ticked by they waited fearfully for the balloon to go up, frustrated in the knowledge that there was not a thing they could do about changing the course of world events.

That summer however defied all the prophets of doom, and Paris continued helterskelter towards eventual armageddon without a care in the world. In June Albert, much to his shame, nearly forgot Barbara's birthday. *'Something I have never done before, and I rang her today, two days late, to ask her forgiveness. Of course being the wonderful sister she is, she told me she quite understood.'*

In July, as the temperature rose, the girls grew all the more desirable and the two young men were swept along by the torrent of *joie de vivre*, so much so that by August Albert's spirits had risen to such an extent that he wrote in his diary: *'I'm beginning to think my dire predictions will never come about.'*

In fact, two more months of living in a fool's paradise slipped by before the blow struck and his growing optimism exploded in his face. For in October Hitler made it quite clear where his ambitions still lay.

'The Germans have invaded the Sudetenland,' announced Josef Milosz, the Ambassador, to the gathered company of diplomats and staff on his customary morning briefing. 'In my opinion, however, the biggest disaster is that we have reoccupied the Zaolsie to protect our southern flank against them, and by the reactions of our so-called friends the French and English I think I may be proved right.'

A round little man of fifty-nine, with receding hair and bad sight, Josef looked over his spectacles at the now silent company. 'I think I need not tell you that this does not look good for our poor country and because I feel we may soon be facing a crisis I must cancel all leave. I'm very sorry for those of you who have not been home for some time but I'm sure you will understand. I hope I'm being too cautious, and if so, you will soon be able to get away again. I fear this will put back all your leave, as the timetable has now been disrupted, and those of you who had hoped to go home for Christmas or the New Year will have to give way to others.'

He shrugged. 'That, ladies and gentlemen, is the cost you must pay for being in the service of your country on a foreign soil. I know you are all worried about families and friends back home so I suggest you contact them and say that leave has been put on hold. No need to alarm them too much, as we must hope this crisis will be only temporary.'

'I was surprised how depressed I felt, as Andre and I left the Ambassador's office,' wrote Albert later that day. *'I have been looking forward to going home for the New Year, and now that bastard Hitler has put his foot into my plans. Damn him! And I have just struck a bet with Andre that we won't get home before war breaks out. I must ring father tomorrow. He will, of course, understand why I can't get home, but I'm sure he will be distressed by the apparent worsening of the European situation, especially as I think I may have been raising his hopes a little too much just recently.'*

And the next day he wrote: *'Father has taken the news calmly, saying that he had expected me to call with bad news, and that I had been sounding just a bit too optimistic recently. Especially as the radio in Poland had been full of nothing else but Hitler's reoccupation of the Sudetenland. Then he ended by asking me if I thought this could be the beginning of my scenario? Trying to sound cheerful I told him that I doubted it very much, but I was not surprised when he refused to accept my assurances, and replied that he had decided not to let Mieszki Wielkie be plundered by the Germans or by hordes of Bolsheviks! I feel much happier now that he has taken my warnings seriously, and it is good to know that he will be sending some of the more valuable treasures to Paris.*

'If my talk with father went smoothly, it most certainly didn't with mother. She was obviously most distressed that I would not be coming home and I have to confess that it was a great relief when she handed over to Barbara. In fact she was not in a much better state, pouring out her concern for the peasants on the estate. This is understandable, as the poor devils have no means of escape, short of leaving what little they have and walking off into the unknown and becoming displaced persons. My God, I must be thankful that a route out of Poland is available if my family choose to use it. Once more it brings home to me the inequality that exists in our society. But when all is said and done, I'm as selfish as the next man and I told Barbara that it was no time to think of others. She must look after herself and be sure that father moves quickly when the time comes. Oh God, how I love them all. Then, as I was just about to end our conversation she tells me that she has been to a dance and met a major in

the infantry. She is obviously smitten by him, although he must be years older. I fear that all those years in a Convent may have made my little sister very vulnerable to a man's charm, and rather too impetuous. I wish I was there to guide her, and to tell her that she has all the time in the world to choose a decent man, and not to jump into the first man's arms who smiles at her – father and mother will be quite useless. I can only hope that the major is honourable.'

After several weeks the uneasy calm of the past few months returned to the Embassy, as Europe once more seemed to hold its breath and settle down as if nothing had happened. By December the normally cautious Josef felt it was safe to allow a few of his staff back to Poland for Christmas. As expected Albert and Andre were not amongst them and Albert was all the more disappointed as by that time his sister's letters were full of nothing but the wonders of Major Kasimir Malczewski. *'I'm worried, but can do nothing except suggest caution,'* Albert wrote, *'I must not sound too severe or I will only accelerate her desire.'*

The two friends spent the holiday on routine work at the Embassy and monumental binges at night. *'I can't remember,'* wrote Albert, *'when I have ever had such a recurring hangover, which only aggravates my feeling of gloom. I never thought I would miss going home so much.'*

Eventually, during one of his telephone conversations with his sister, he confessed his feelings to her. 'It's bad enough being cooped up here without feeling the hand of death on my shoulder all day.'

'Oh, Albert, what a thing to say – I worry endlessly about you as it is.'

Realising he had been selfish he immediately tried to rectify his mistake. 'I'm sorry, I shouldn't have said that. I can't think what came over me. Bloody stupid! Please, please try to forget I ever said it.'

He thought he could hear her crying. 'Barbara, are you there?'

'Yes, yes. Just catching my breath. Don't worry, I understand how you feel, but don't say that sort of thing to mother, will you?'

'Of course not.'

He ended the conversation abruptly – slamming down the receiver in disgust. That night he wrote: *'How could I have been so damned insensitive? What a stupid thing to say to her.'*

And a week later when he rang again he could hear the tension in his sister's voice.

He voiced his frustration to Andre, who put an arm on his friend's shoulder. 'Don't fuss so much. She realises we are all under great stress, and probably she is pleased that you can confide in her.'

'Maybe, but it would have been more tactful to have kept my mouth shut.'

'Well, you can't do anything about it now, so cheer up, and after work let's go down to that little café opposite the Louvre, where we met those girls the other night, and get drunk.'

Albert shook his head. 'Sorry, drink will only depress me further. You can go without me this time.'

That night Albert wrote: *'I have upset him. After all, he was only trying to help. I just want to be on my own.'*

His mood was indicative of how the younger members of the Embassy staff were feeling, and Josef was not slow to sense the atmosphere of frustration and restlessness. So he decided to hold a party to herald in the New Year. Privately he felt it might well be the last one he gave in Paris and so he was determined that if the lights were to go out at the Embassy he would throw a party few of his fellow diplomats would forget.

Good as his word, the champagne flowed and nearly two hundred guests danced and ate from 10.00 p.m. until well into the first morning of 1939. Two days later when Josef summoned all the staff into his office to give them a run down on events, as had become his practice, he was pleased to note a much more cheerful atmosphere. That night when he sat down to dinner with his wife Zofia he expressed his pleasure.

'It was worth all the money, my dear. You should have seen the staff this morning – completely different. I even got a smile out of young Mieszkowski.'

Zofia looked lovingly across the table. She had become a Milosz when only eighteen and had never regretted it. True, there had been some disappointments over the thirty years of their marriage, especially her inability to have children. However, Josef's life as a diplomat had softened her sadness and she considered herself lucky to have travelled with him to so many countries before taking up his first Ambassadorial post in London and then finally on to Paris where she felt his career might well be drawing to a close. For, regardless of the turmoil in Europe, she knew his eyesight was failing badly and feared that soon he would be blind.

'Ah, yes, young Albert. I feel so sorry for him, Josef. I expect he is worried sick about his beautiful home.'

She had been born in Lvov and known Mieszki Wielkie and Albert's grandparents quite well, and had met Josef at one of the many magnificent balls that the Mieszkowskis threw each year.

Josef nodded. 'I'm sure you are right, my dear, and I can understand his feelings. But don't forget, Albert is not the only one who has left a lovely home and family behind, though I must admit he seems to be the most affected. Ah, well, I'm afraid he will just have to grin and bear it like the rest of them.'

He picked up his wine glass, held it up to the light and smiled. 'Those were happy days, weren't they? What it was to dance in that glorious house and be in love with someone so beautiful. No young woman could hold a candle to you. I can still remember it as if it were yesterday as you came down that long hall towards me in that dark green dress with your hair falling down onto your shoulders. It was your eyes that really conquered me – the blueness and the excitement that flashed from them. My God, how could I ever forget! You were magnificent!'

He twirled his glass and laughed. 'I was a lucky man. You had many suitors, didn't you?'

Zofia smiled contentedly. 'Maybe, but you won my heart immediately.'

'In spite of being shorter than most?'

'That never worried me. You danced divinely and gave me your undivided attention that night. And then, as I got to know you better and our relationship flourished, I found a character that I could really understand and appreciate – what an aphrodisiac I found that to be. However, it was your absolute conviction that one day you would be an Ambassador that put the icing on the cake. You see, I too was ambitious!'

'I told you that I was going to be an Ambassador? How damned conceited! I can't remember that.'

'Almost before you said I was beautiful!'

'My God! And you married me even so!'

'From the moment we walked down the aisle together hand-in-hand and I felt you trembling I knew I had done the right thing. You were, and still are, an exceptional man, and I have never stopped loving you.'

Josef brushed a tear off a cheek and took a long drink of his Château Talbot, before replying. 'Luckily I can look you straight in the eye and say the same. Love is a funny old thing, but like this wine it grows better as time moves on. We may be growing old and the future may look bleak, but nothing can take away the years that we have enjoyed together.'

Zofia touched her face. 'Oh, come now, we are not old yet; I can still feel the smoothness of my skin. A few odd wrinkles, I grant you, and not such firm bosoms, but we have years ahead of us yet.'

Josef put his glass down and stared at his wife. 'I did not mean to cast aspersions on your beauty, my dear. As far as I'm concerned, you have not changed one little bit since the evening I first kissed you. But have we got years left to enjoy? I wonder. The world is trembling on the brink of an abyss and who knows what horrors lie ahead. Hitler, I fear, will not be easy to stop, and if and when he is, will Europe be the same? Will Russia leave Poland alone? Will Germany be allowed to exist as she does now, or will a terrible vengeance fall upon her? And if Hitler is triumphant? What then? We certainly won't be sitting here drinking rare claret; more likely we will be dead or refugees walking aimlessly around a captive and submissive Europe.'

'Oh, Josef, what an outlook!' cried Zofia. 'How can you be so depressing? I'm sure everything will work out. I have a great belief that good always conquers evil in the end. We may not be able to enjoy the coming years as much, and hardship may well be around the corner, but we and our country will survive – I truly believe that.' Then she held out her empty glass. 'Just in case I'm wrong, let's drink to those wonderful years and forget the future for tonight at least.'

She got up from the table and walked slowly towards him. 'Come on, let's take this wine to bed and relive some of those marvellous moments as well!'

He chuckled and pulled her down onto his knee and kissed the nape of her neck. He could taste the familiar fragrance of her scent on his tongue. She had never changed it from the moment they had first met and it still sent shivers down his spine. He closed his eyes and felt for her breasts. 'Is that a challenge, my dear?'

'It's whatever you want to make of it?' she whispered, as she put her glass down on the table and reached up to ruffle his hair.

On 22 March 1939 Germany delivered its ultimatum to Poland, demanding that Danzig should become part of the Third Reich, and the Polish government rejected the demand outright. When, a week later, Great Britain offered an unconditional guarantee of Polish territorial integrity, followed up in early April by the signing of a full military alliance between herself, France and Poland, Josef felt that Hitler would strike at his country sooner rather than later.

Once more the staff at the Embassy held their breath, but when three months had passed without Josef's dire predictions coming true, some even dared to think that yet again their country had stood up to the bully and won. Josef continued however to advise caution, party as he was to secret information coming out of Germany that totally contradicted the mood of optimism.

In August, when he was briefed on a supposedly secret deal signed by Ribbentrop and Molotov on behalf of their two countries on the future of

Poland, he was convinced that there was only a short spell of peace left before his country was torn apart.

Even he could never have guessed how this was to come about.

Chapter 3

On the evening of 31 August a dozen German convicts were dressed up as Polish soldiers and ordered to attack a German radio station in Gleiwitz, Upper Silesia. The next morning a startled world woke to the remarkable news that Poland had attacked the Third Reich and that its soldiers had invaded Poland in defence of the Fatherland.

At seven o'clock that same morning Josef hastily called an emergency meeting of his staff and, unshaven and feeling very shaky without his usual breakfast cup of strong black coffee, broke the news to them.

'It has begun, ladies and gentlemen – we are at war with Germany. All leave is cancelled and this Embassy is now on a war footing and everyone will sleep here from now on. We will use the ballroom for the men and the small drawing room for the ladies. It is indeed a sad day. Long live Poland!'

Two days later, on 3 September, Britain and France declared war on Germany and on 5 September Albert and Andre were summoned into the Ambassador's office.

'Please sit down, gentlemen.' Josef waved absently at two chairs on the other side of his desk. He looked pale and drawn.

'I have here a letter from General Anders in Warsaw – actually, perhaps I should say, an order.'

He looked across his desk to make sure he had their attention.

'It is ordering you to Warsaw immediately to remove the gold bullion from the Polish State Bank and take it to Trieste for loading onto a British destroyer bound for the United States of America.'

There was a stunned silence in the room.

'*I remember Andre recovering first,*' wrote Albert.

'They want us to do what?' asked Andre.

23

'Take Poland's gold bullion to America. Otherwise it will almost certainly fall into the hands of the Germans.'

'Why us?' asked Albert.

'It seems you are well thought of by quite a number of high-ranking officers – you apparently impressed them with your initiative while you were at the cavalry school at Kracow. And you, Andre, I gather know the Tatra range of mountains especially well from your mountaineering holidays and they seem to think that you will have to cross them to reach Budapest.'

'Oh!' injected a surprised Andre.

Josef looked over his spectacles. 'Well, that's what they say, young man. Added to which they think you both will be able to enlist help from the men on your estates and that once across the border your diplomatic status may help.'

Andre still looked puzzled. 'Surely such an important and dangerous job would be better done by men who are professional soldiers?'

'They seem to think they can't spare anyone,' said Josef with little conviction.

'Why the Tatras?' asked Andre. 'They are not the quickest route to Trieste and are noted for their deplorable weather. It could be suicide taking the gold that way.'

Josef looked at the letter on his desk. 'The reason why you will have to cross the Tatras and go through Budapest is that the Germans have invaded us from three fronts, and already all other routes are blocked. Their advance has been devastatingly quick, I know, but they have God knows how many tanks and planes and literally millions of men. What hope have we got? And where are our brave Allies, you may well ask.'

His tone was bitter. 'All they have done so far is make noises and drop leaflets over a few German cities. God in heaven, what use, I ask you, is that? Apparently there is no sign of any French troop movement. If something doesn't happen soon we will be overrun. We already have been forced back to the Vistula and Bzura rivers and I'm getting reports through that Kracow is in danger of falling.'

'Kracow! My God!' said an appalled Albert.

Josef shook his head. 'Unbelievable, I agree – but it highlights our terrible predicament. If we can't hold the line on the Vistula we will withdraw to an area around Lvov where at least we will have our backs to neutral Russia and a friendly Roumania.'

'I asked him how long he thought Russia would stay neutral,' Albert wrote.

'You think like me, young man,' said Josef, allowing himself to smile. 'Let's hope we are wrong. Now, back to the point. There can be no argument. You must leave immediately for your estates to recruit your men and then go on to Warsaw. It says in the letter you will need at least forty men and it would help if they could drive. Gentlemen, General Anders exhorts you to move swiftly – you have little time.'

Albert looked enquiringly at Josef. 'Forty men? That seems a hell of a lot.'

'I agree. However, that is what the letter says. You must realise that the value of the gold is enormous.'

'Have you any idea how much?' asked Andre.

'Not really. But I know it comes to millions of dollars.'

'Dear God!' exclaimed Albert, 'And we are expected to cart it across half of bloody Europe with peasants from our estates. It is beginning to sound quite exciting!'

'God, how exhilarated I felt!' wrote Albert later. *'I had resigned myself to a frustrating time at the Embassy while all my compatriots were fighting and dying for their country. Now out of the blue myself and Andre had been given a thoroughly dangerous task. It was an immense challenge, but the bonus was that I would see Mieszki Wielkie and my family again. I was prepared to risk anything for that alone. I looked across at Andre. He was obviously as excited as I was at having the chance of actively serving his country. We will do it, I said rather stupidly, for of course we had no choice.'*

'Well, I don't think you would have been able to decline,' said Josef, a faint smile on his lips as he pushed back his chair. 'A military plane is waiting for you outside Paris. My driver and car are at your disposal. You will fly to Kracow where you are to pick up two officers who have been instructed to give you all the assistance they can, and then carry on to your estates. I have arranged for a sum of money to be made available for you which you can collect from my secretary before you leave. It therefore only remains for me to wish you luck, gentlemen, and I hope that when we next meet it will be in happier times. You might well find this useful to take with you.'

He held out a blue envelope to Albert. As he took it Albert looked at him enquiringly.

'A letter from General Anders ordering you to report to him immediately in Warsaw. No mention of the gold, of course, just in case it falls into the wrong hands, but he thinks it could be helpful as a sort of pass in case you meet obstacles on the way.'

'I understand, sir,' said Albert, holding out his hand. 'And I would like to wish you luck here.'

Andre nodded. 'Most certainly. I would like to add my thanks for all your kindness.'

The three of them shook hands before the two men made for the door.

'One moment.' They stopped and turned to face Josef again.

He was vigorously polishing his glasses. 'Do you know, I envy you two. If I was your age I would be itching to get into the fight. Safe journey, now.'

Albert could have sworn his eyes were damp. 'I am sure you would do a better job than us, sir.'

Josef rammed his glasses back on his nose. 'Ha! Don't try and flatter me young man! I am just too old and blind.'

The two men laughed uneasily.

'Go on, off with you,' Josef snorted. He looked away and started rummaging amongst the papers on his desk.

It was a familiar way that he used for dismissal and they hurried out of the room, but once on the landing Andre turned to his friend. 'Poor old bugger. You know, I really think he would like to be in our shoes. I hope he survives the war so that we can tell him how we got on.'

Albert shook his head. 'I should think our chances are about even.'

Andre looked surprised. 'Why do you say that? Surely he will be safe here?'

'Not if Germany invades the rest of Europe and occupies Paris. Frankly, I wouldn't think Hitler was the type to worry about anyone's diplomatic immunity.'

'What a bastard! Do you know, I think I would rather be killed fighting than be put into some camp to rot away from disease or starvation.'

'I agree,' said Albert. 'I just hope the old man gets away before the Hun catches him. He deserves more than years watching himself grow old in some stinking camp parted from his wife. However, I doubt if we will have much time to think of him – we are going to need a fair slice of luck ourselves, you know, for unless I am very mistaken we have got a tricky job on our hands.'

'I think that might be an understatement,' said Andre. 'What do you think our chances are?'

'I don't know. Time is obviously not going to be on our side. Therefore I would have thought it sensible for us to split up when we reach Kracow. No point in following each other to our respective estates. I suggest that you fly to Lodz with one of the officers to collect your men and I will go with the other one to Mieszki Wielkie and do the same. Then we can meet in Warsaw. That way we will at least be saving some time. What do you say, eh?'

'A good idea. In that case we must decide how many men we each try to recruit.'

'I think the question is going to be how many able and trustworthy men are going to be left on our estates. To be honest, even in normal times I don't think I would trust more than a handful. I just can't see us getting over forty. So I suggest we bring as many good men as we can muster and if we have too many when we arrive in Warsaw we will have to send some of them home.

'Very well.'

Albert put a hand on Andre's shoulder. 'I think we are going to need more than just a little luck!'

Andre chuckled. 'You can say that again! Who would have thought you and I would ever be given the responsibility of getting Poland's wealth out of the way of the thieving Germans! I think we face quite an adventure.'

Albert roared with laughter. 'Another one of your understatements, I suspect!'

The two men hurried off to pack their suitcases and Albert to write his diary. His last paragraph read: *'I feel very frightened as I sit here in the safety of the Embassy, because we have been given a task of great responsibility. I seriously wonder if we are up to it. Only time will tell. This will be the last entry for some while as I have decided to leave my diary behind. I wouldn't want it to fall into German hands. In case I'm killed I will ask Josef to send it to my parents if they are still alive.'*

Josef promised he would carry out Albert's wishes.

They flew to Prague first, where they were met at the airport by a Polish attaché with directions of where to land outside Kracow, and a warning not to cross into Polish airspace until just before dawn. That way, they were told, was their best chance of avoiding any marauding Luftwaffe pilots.

They looked at each other and smiled – it would be a bit of an anticlimax to be shot out of the sky before they even reached Warsaw. But they need not have worried, for the night was pitch black and the pilot had done it several times before; and at 4.00 a.m. on 6 September they arrived at a small airfield outside Kracow with nothing worse than frozen bones to show for their dash across the hostile skies.

As they urged their cramped limbs out of the plane, two shadowy figures hurried towards them.

'The two officers from Paris?' asked one.

'Yes,' stammered Albert through frozen lips, screwing up his eyes in an attempt to see their faces, for he was sure he had recognised the voice.

'Good. Then follow us, please.'

They fell into step behind the two men and after a short walk they were ushered into a large barn. By the smell, it had not long been vacated by sheep. At the far end a kerosene light was burning and a soldier was bending over a crackling radio. When they reached the light Albert looked curiously at the faces of their two hosts.

'Well I'll be damned, Bartek Zablocki! I thought I recognised your voice out there.'

Bartek hesitated for only a second as he surveyed Albert's shaking figure. 'Of course it's Mieszkowski! Good God! Albert Mieszkowski! For security reasons I was not given your names.' He laughed happily as he turned to his companion. 'Albert and I spent many a night out in the cold on some bloody exercise sharing our coffee and talking over our hopes for the future. But he didn't stay a soldier. Took to diplomacy instead. Fat lot of good that's done us!'

He laughed again. 'Who is your friend?'

Albert turned to Andre. 'You know him – Andre Zaluski. He was on the same course as us.'

Bartek screwed up his nose. 'Of course. Hello, Andre. Sorry I didn't recognise you. But then, I never shared a trench with you! This is Marek Radziwill.'

Marek raised a hand and Bartek slapped Albert on the back and pointed to the radio. 'Bad news, I'm afraid. Kracow will almost certainly fall tomorrow. We are fighting a losing battle and the feeling of the Generals is that we should withdraw to other positions rather than allow the town and its inhabitants to be destroyed.'

Albert sucked in his breath. 'We heard in Paris that the news was bad. To be honest, we didn't quite believe it. How could the Germans have got so far after only five days?'

'Devastating weaponry, superior arms and millions of men,' Bartek replied. 'We never stood a chance and unless you get out of here quickly your war will be over before it has begun.'

Albert looked puzzled. 'We were told that you and Marek were coming with us to Warsaw.'

'So we were. However, our orders have been changed. We have got to go back into Kracow and help organise the retreat. You are on your own, I'm afraid, and you can't even have the plane. Our need here is greater than yours and, as I'm sure you appreciate, planes are not the easiest things to find just at the moment! So all I can offer you is a car, a drum of fuel and a thermos of coffee.'

Albert swallowed and glanced at Andre before turning back to Bartek. 'Do you know we are supposed to go to our estates first and recruit some men?'

'I was just coming to that. That order is cancelled, because the fear is that Warsaw will have fallen before you get there. Already most of the west and north of the country is in enemy hands but the road from here to Warsaw via Radom is clear. However I must warn you that things are changing almost by the minute and reports are now getting pretty vague as our communications get destroyed.'

Albert pulled a face. 'Well, this sounds really great. We're half-frozen, can't have you, the plane or our men. What are we expected to do? Take the gold out on our own? Dear God, we are not magicians!'

Bartek shrugged resignedly. 'I know that. But they are right, it would be sheer folly for you both to go to your estates first. The sooner you get to Warsaw the better. At the moment we are holding the road from the west to Lodz but if that falls then it cannot be long before the Germans are outside the city. They are already bombing it heavily.'

He turned to Andre. 'Where is your home?'

Andre wasn't sure he wanted to tell him for at the mention of Lodz he had already guessed what he was going to say.

'Ostrow,' he said quietly.

Bartek shook his head. 'Well, that would be out for a start. We heard it was in German hands yesterday. I'm sorry – I really am.'

Andre went white as a sheet. 'Oh God, I wonder what has happened to my parents.'

Bartek patted his arm. 'If they had any sense they will have fled across the border to Czechoslovakia or Hungary. Who knows, if you get to Trieste you may run into them.'

Andre gave a weak smile. 'Pigs may fly! To be honest, at this moment I wouldn't give any of us much of a chance of living for long. Especially Albert and I if we have to take the route I think we will have to.'

'Indeed not,' said Bartek. 'I suppose you can only go through the mountains now and then on to Budapest. I agree it will be very difficult, especially if you have the Germans on your tails by then.'

He put his hands on his hips. 'Well, this conversation is only depressing us. It's straight to Warsaw and the State Bank for you and Kracow for me and Marek. Now I must telephone the Bank and tell them you are on your way.'

He saw Albert glance at his watch. 'Don't worry, no one leaves the Bank these days.'

It seemed to Albert to take an eternity before the connection with the Bank was made and Bartek was speaking to the Governor. He spoke briefly and to the point.

'Your men are here, sir, and about to leave by car. As you know, they can't have the plane. I suggest you give them twenty-four hours and if by then they haven't arrived, make other plans.'

There was a moment's silence as the Governor replied.

'Very well, sir, I will tell them. Goodbye.'

Bartek put the receiver down and turned to Albert. 'He wishes you luck. I must admit I think he would be wiser to use men already in Warsaw, but I gather that along with other reasons, which no doubt have already been explained to you, he is convinced your diplomatic status may help when you get across the border and arrive in Trieste.'

Albert grimaced. 'Well, I can only hope we won't let him down and that the Germans don't beat us to it!'

'That's a risk you will just have to take,' said Bartek. 'Now, I can see you are still cold, so grab a cup of coffee before you leave. Dawn will be here soon and then the shelling and bombing will begin again.'

They drank from steaming mugs handed to them by Marek and listened carefully to him as he explained how to get onto the right road. 'There are two maps in the car. One of this area and one of Warsaw. You won't get lost once you are on the right road, for all you will have to do is to go the opposite way to the tide of refugees.'

He was interrupted as an explosion rocked the barn and Bartek grabbed at Albert's arm. 'By God, that was close. The bastards must have discovered this airfield. Come on! We have no time to lose!'

As they ran out of the barn Albert noticed a red glow in the sky on his left.

'Kracow?' he asked Bartek.

'No, a village nearby. So far, the damage to Kracow has been slight. Even so, it is pretty terrible in there. We can't treat the wounded or bury the dead. All we can hope for is a bit of compassion from the Germans when they arrive.'

Albert didn't think it was the right moment to say that he doubted he would get that. Instead he stared at the outline of the car parked outside the barn.

Bartek guessed what he was thinking. 'That's yours, Albert. Old and battered, but I am assured the best we have left.'

Albert took a closer look at the car. 'It does go, does it?'

Bartek chuckled. 'Oh yes. The engine is in first class order.'

Albert laughed. 'Well, in that case we are bound to be okay. What does it matter if the chassis falls off on the way!'

It was an attempt to ease the tension but in fact it did the very opposite and just heightened his awareness of the dangers he faced. He felt his stomach screw up and he grabbed for Andre's arm. 'Christ, come on, man, let's get out of here. I'll drive first.'

Years later when he was reunited with his diary he had no difficulty in remembering his feelings as he climbed into the car. He wrote: *'I remember feeling sick with fear. I think it must have been the unknown that beckoned beyond the airfield. Nor had I ever had to face such potential danger. It suddenly dawned on me that my life was at risk. I would have liked to have stayed with Bartek and Marek and taken my chances fighting the Germans. I looked across at Andre as he got into the seat beside me. He was a shadowy figure in the dawn light, but I could have sworn I smelt his fear!'*

'Oh damn!' Albert cried as, with eyes fixed firmly in front of him, he pressed the starter and slammed the car into gear. He knew that to glance at Bartek would be a severe test of his willpower. The barn was like a magnet. Not until there was no danger of seeing Bartek or the barn did he want to look back.

Only when they had reached the road did he turn to Andre again. 'Sorry about that, but for a moment there I was in a blue funk.'

'You have no need to apologise to me,' said Andre, reaching for the map that lay on the seat between them. 'I was just the same.' He was silent for a moment. 'Do you think we will ever see those two again?'

'Only God knows the answer to that, and all I can say is that I am bloody glad I can't ask Him!'

Chapter 4

It was not long before they discovered how right Marek was – the roads were packed with the flotsam of war. Women, children and old men pushed their meagre belongings along in front of them, all heading to God knows where. The two men found it a thoroughly demoralising experience and the tales that some of the refugees told them made them realise that no Pole could expect pity from Hitler's barbarous hordes of murderers. They heard of atrocity after atrocity, especially towards the Jews, that left them gasping for breath and wanting to close their ears to the savage tales that they were told. However, there was no escaping the truth and as the day wore on the more horrific the stories seemed to become.

If they had any remaining doubts about Hitler's intentions it was quickly dispelled that evening when they came upon two middle aged women with a harrowing story of the Germans' brutality in their village west of Lodz.

As soon as the village had been overrun all the males that could be found, irrespective of age, had been herded into the little square and shot. Two of the men that died were their husbands. That however had not been the end of their nightmare, for no sooner was the warm blood of their menfolk staining the cobbles of the square than they had been picked up and interrogated for hours by a German officer who had boasted that it was Hitler's intention to exterminate not only the Jews but the whole Polish nation. It had been a terrifying ordeal and they had been certain that they were the next to be shot. But much to their surprise, six hours later, they had been released on the understanding that they did not remain in the village.

'What was the point of that?' asked Albert.

One of the women shrugged her shoulders, looked up at him and gave him a weak smile. 'We have no idea. They didn't tell us a thing. Just kicked us out like cattle to fend for ourselves. It matters little – we have nothing to live for – to be honest, death would be a relief. No doubt, however, we will keep going until we drop or are killed by the Germans. It is surprising how strong the will to live is.'

'I'm so sorry,' mumbled Andre, 'We can't even offer you a lift.'

'Don't worry yourself about that, young man,' said the taller of the two women. 'I think you will have enough on your plate soon without having to worry about two old biddies.'

She raised her hand and was gone – swallowed up with her companion in the mass of humanity jamming the road.

'It makes you feel sick, doesn't it?' Andre said.

'It's really better not to think about it,' said Albert. 'There is damn all we can do to help.'

That proved to be the last time they were able to stop and talk to anybody. For at 3.00 a.m. on the second day, 7 September, with the fires burning in Warsaw lighting up the sky ahead of them, enemy aircraft started straafing the long line of refugees. It would have been sensible for them to have driven off the road whenever an attack came but there was no time for that – they were already behind schedule.

As yet another wave of fighters came over, Andre shouted to Albert, 'Better to die trying to get there on time than to arrive too late and find out that we have been through this hell for bloody nothing!'

Not really sure of his friend's logic, Albert just nodded.

The luck that Albert so badly wanted was with them. And although they hadn't slept or eaten since leaving the airfield they felt a certain elation as they arrived in the suburbs of Warsaw, covered in dirt and on the verge of exhaustion, at 5.00 a.m. It was going to be a close run thing to make the Bank within the twenty-four hour deadline, but they were relatively confident, having survived so far.

Their euphoria was to be short-lived.

'Dear God!' exclaimed Albert as he stopped the car by a road junction and surveyed the utter destruction in front of him. The whole road was blocked by wrecked vehicles and masonry and glass from nearby buildings, and the ear-shattering noise of a nearby explosion only served to heighten his awareness of the dangerous situation they were in, and that the streets of Warsaw were every bit as dangerous as the roads outside.

'This must be worse than Hell,' he shouted above the noise.

Andre did not answer. He was crying silently into his hands as he realised what his family must have gone through.

Albert dug him in the ribs. 'Come on! Where to now?' He had not been to Warsaw more than half a dozen times and although on two of those visits he had gone to the State Bank with his father, the destruction made it very difficult for him to recognise anything.

'Sorry,' murmured Andre bending over the map. 'Looks blocked here, so turn left and then carry on until you reach a bridge. Then I think you turn right. That should take us into the centre and the Bank should be somewhere there. That is, if it's still standing!'

Albert swung the car left, weaving around rubble and groups of dazed people just standing in the middle of the road. They hardly seemed to notice the car as it passed them. Even above the noise of the car's engine they could hear the constant crump of bombs exploding. It was proving a nerve-wracking journey and several times when they saw buildings in front of them disappear in balls of flame they felt they weren't going to make it.

Make it they did – although it took three hours to reach the centre. By the time Albert swung the car into a wide street which Andre assured him housed the State Bank they were both thoroughly irritating each other and suffering from cracking headaches. All this was forgotten as Andre gave a shout.

'There it is! And, by God, still standing!'

It looked a little scarred but stood proudly, almost defiantly, amongst all the devastation.

Albert skidded to a halt by the Bank entrance and rested his head on the steering wheel. He was shaking so badly that he knew if he got out too quickly his legs would crumple underneath him.

He glanced across at Andre. 'All right?'

'Nothing that twenty-four hours sleep and a good meal wouldn't cure.' He opened his door and looked out. 'Let's go and see if we still have a job!'

Albert gingerly lowered his feet to the ground and held on to the side of the car, just in case his legs refused to hold his weight.

He looked round as Andre joined him. 'Christ, I feel shaky!'

'Not surprising. You have done most of the driving and I shouldn't think we have stopped for longer than half an hour at any one time. It's a bloody miracle we are still standing!'

'And alive,' said Albert, letting go of the car and taking a hesitant step towards the Bank.

On the Bank steps two soldiers and an officer barred their way. The officer looked them up and down suspiciously. Although covered in dust and unshaven like most of the men in Warsaw he couldn't quite understand why they were looking so uncertain.

He drew his pistol. 'The Bank is closed. So move along please.'

Albert drew out Anders' letter from his trouser pocket. 'Here, I haven't the time or the energy to argue, just read this.'

The officer read it – looked up – read it again and then waved his pistol. 'If you are who this letter says then you are expected. Have you any other identification? I can't be too careful, you know.'

'Of course we understand,' said Albert. 'Here is my diplomatic passport. Does that satisfy you?'

The officer held out his hand to Andre. 'Yours, please.'

Once he had both their passports he raised a hand. 'Wait here.' He went to the door and disappeared, returning in five minutes in a much more cheerful mood. 'You are most welcome; these passports really cheered them up in there.' He handed them back with the letter. 'Please come this way, gentlemen.'

They followed him through the door and into a high-ceilinged hall full of troops, and on into a large room with the shutters drawn. It was almost dark. Two single lamps were fighting a losing battle to light the whole area and they had difficulty in making out five men sitting round a long table. Three were in uniform, the other two wore suits. One of these, a tall white-haired man, rose from his chair and came towards them with his hand held out.

'Welcome, gentlemen. I can't tell you how glad we are to see you. We were beginning to think that you were not going to make it.'

'We had our doubts at times, sir,' replied Albert.

'I'm sure, I'm sure. Now come over to the table where we can see you better and we can introduce ourselves. Time is of the essence, so please forgive me if I appear abrupt.'

Once they reached the table the white-haired man pointed at two empty chairs either side of him.

'Please sit down.' He waited a moment. 'I am Jacub Slowacki, Governor of the State Bank. The man on my right is Jan Mickiewicz, my assistant. In clockwise order are Generals Anders, Mielecki and Murat. It is General Mielecki whom I think you will both know.'

Albert and Andre nodded to each in turn. It had been some time since they had seen Mielecki – he'd been Commandant of the Cavalry School during their time there. Albert thought he had aged.

'Right,' said Jacub Slowacki. 'Before we get down to the business that you were summoned here for I think I should tell you gentlemen that we have just heard Kracow has fallen and that means it cannot be long before the Germans are beating on our door.'

'Dear God!' exclaimed Albert. 'I had a friend there.'

General Anders spoke for the first time. 'Ah yes, Bartek Zablocki. He and Marek Radziwill should have come with you. I'm afraid we have had no news from them for about eight hours now. I can tell you, however, that they were back in Kracow by the time they went off the air and that means that if everything has gone according to plan they could have survived. We hoped to pull out what remained of our forces in the city without too many more casualties.'

Albert nodded. 'I see, sir.'

Jacub Slowacki looked concerned. 'The fall of Kracow makes it all the more urgent for you to get the gold out of here and reach Trieste. Perhaps a Russian port would have been easier but I am sure I do not have to explain why that option is not available. I'm afraid to say that your route to Trieste changes nearly every minute, but it looks as if you will have to cross the Carpathians somewhere near Mukacevo as the Germans are cutting off all your routes further west. At the moment, providing you go east to Lublin and then on to Lvov, you should reach the mountains without much difficulty. As you know, we decided that time had become so urgent that you should come directly here instead of going first to your estates. This has caused quite a problem, as now that we must find all the drivers, the Generals here feel that they cannot spare you a large escort. So I suggest that as you are going to Lvov it might be worth your while, Mieszkowski, going on to your estate and trying to collect some reliable men as an extra guard. We hope you won't need to fight but you will be carrying a fortune in gold, and people do talk, and it will be difficult for you to travel unnoticed. Around the twentieth of this month a British destroyer arrives in Trieste to take the gold to America. If you are not there when he arrives, the Captain has orders to wait for you for one week only. After you have completed your operation you are both to report to our Embassy in Budapest.'

'What if we don't make it by then?' asked Andre.

'I think we can assume the gold lost and that you are either dead or prisoners,' said Slowacki. 'However, if by some rare chance you do get through after the destroyer has sailed it has been arranged with our Embassy that they will contact the British Ambassador. Some new arrangements can then be made.'

'How much gold is there?' asked Andre.

'The total amount comes to three hundred million dollars.'

'My God!' exclaimed Andre.

'Three hundred million dollars!' repeated Albert in amazement. 'We are going to need a few lorries to carry that lot! I should think we will be noticed!'

Jacub Slowacki raised a hand. 'You will, in fact, only be taking out half that amount. We just haven't the transport to carry it all. As it is you will have a convoy of nearly seventy trucks. It would have been less if we could have got hold of three-tonners but unfortunately that was not possible, so you have got one-tonners instead.'

'What will you do with the rest of the gold?' asked Albert.

'Try and get it out later, or even hide it here in Warsaw. We were trying to think of something when you arrived.'

Albert frowned. 'I see. My God, seventy trucks. We will stand out like a sore thumb. The Luftwaffe will spot us miles away.'

General Anders nodded. 'I think that will only be the case early on. Our reports say that there is no air activity by the Germans very far east of Warsaw. If you leave here tonight the chances are you will be well away from their area of activity by dawn. If not, then I accept you will be a very long column and could attract attention. You must hope that as you will be mixed in with the refugees they will give you some cover. Not that that will make much difference – we hear that the Germans are being pretty indiscriminate in their attacks.'

'We are too well aware of that already,' said Andre.

Anders shrugged. 'Well, there you are then – success will depend on your luck and initiative, that is one of the reasons we sent for you. I cannot stress too strongly how important it is to get this gold to America. God willing, the Germans will be defeated one day and then perhaps Poland will see peace again. Those of us who are left will have to rebuild this country and we can't do that on a song and a prayer.'

'Andre and I will do our best, sir – that is all we can say,' said Albert.

Anders smiled. 'I'm sure you will. Now I suggest you go and get some food and, I suspect, some much needed sleep. There is a shelter beneath this building where you will be relatively safe from bombs and you can rest until dark. I will make sure you have two uniforms before you leave, as it would be unwise to risk capture in civilian clothes and you will find it easier to give orders. You will have seventy army drivers and an escort of twenty men. I would have liked one for each vehicle but as you have already heard, that is not possible.'

'The gold will start being loaded at eight o'clock tonight,' said Slowacki. 'You should be able to leave about an hour later. Let us hope that we don't get a direct hit before then!' He paused. 'I think, gentlemen, that is all. My assistant Jan Mielecki will take you to the shelter and see that you get food, a wash and a decent bed. I apologise in advance for the quality of the meal, but we are getting short of one or two things.'

The meeting broke up then, the three Generals leaving first, followed by Jacub Slowacki who assured Andre and Albert that he would see them later that evening. Once he had closed the door Jan Mielecki turned to the two men.

'Right, gentlemen, if you would follow me I will take you to food and a bed.'

By nine o'clock that evening the trucks were loaded. Sixty-five of them held the gold, packed tightly into specially made wooden crates designed to fit into the backs of the small one-ton trucks. The other five were packed with food, water, fuel and a meagre supply of ammunition for the forty-odd rifles that they were taking with them. The lack of arms and the shortage of ammunition worried Slowacki, but when he voiced his concern that all the men weren't armed he was swiftly told by Anders that they were lucky to have any rifles at all.

Shortly after 9.15 p.m., Albert and Andre, now in the uniforms of cavalry captains, came out onto a side street behind the Bank with Slowacki and Anders and gazed with some apprehension at the long line of trucks parked down the entire length of the street. Albert thought they would make a perfect target for the Luftwaffe once they were on the open road trying to wend their way through the log-jam of refugees. It would be quite a sight to see one hundred and fifty million dollars worth of gold scattered all over the road.

Although nervous at the thought of the journey ahead, the two men felt well rested. They would have liked a shower to have washed off all the dirt of the last two days but water, like food, was a scarce commodity, and they'd had to make do with a bowl of hot water each.

The sky above them was lit by thousands of white and yellow dots as all the surviving anti-aircraft batteries in the city fired optimistically at the shadows of hundreds of planes, and the street was bathed in an eerie light caused by the fires raging nearby. The noise was deafening.

Albert was tempted to ask the General a question. 'How long can you withstand this sort of bombardment, sir?' he shouted.

'As long as there is just one man alive who can fight on,' Anders replied, putting his mouth close to Albert's left ear. 'You see, we have no option. If we try to flee we will be mown down and if we surrender some of us will be tortured before we are all shot. At the same time we will be condemning to death every Jew that lives in Warsaw. We just cannot do that, so we fight until we are all dead.'

He said it so matter of factly that Albert shivered. 'My God, sir, I don't envy you!'

'You won't be here, young man, so don't waste time on feeling sympathy for me or any of the others. Our job is to kill as many Germans as we can, yours is to get to Trieste – nothing else matters.'

Albert was a little stunned by the man's clear-sightedness. Perhaps that was why he was a General. No time for beating about the bush – if a man is going to die then why tell him otherwise! My God . . . He looked hard at the man and could see no emotion in his face. He wasn't sure he could ever appear so untroubled – but then he would never make a General! He would have liked to have known a bit more about Anders, but there was no time. He had to go – run like a frightened rabbit from the enemy and pray continuously that he and Andre completed their mission safely. There seemed little doubt that the odds were stacked against them. He shuffled uneasily. 'Are all the men ready?' he asked.

Anders pointed at a man who had come forward as soon as they had appeared from the Bank and who was now talking to Andre and Slowacki. 'Ask him. I have decided to spare you one officer, Captain Makowski. It will make it easier with the men as he knows them all and they will obey him better than you, I suspect. However, you still remain in command of the mission and he has been told to follow your orders whatever they are. He is a good man – he won't let you down.'

Albert felt a great surge of relief at this piece of news. He had been wondering how the men would react to taking orders from him and Andre.

He stepped across to the Captain and held out a hand. 'Albert Mieszkowski. I see you two have already met.'

The Captain smiled. 'And I'm Lech Makowski.' He waved at the trucks. 'We have an interesting task at hand. I never thought I would be in charge of so much wealth!' He laughed lightly and Albert immediately warmed to him.

'Nor I. In fact a daunting responsibility. Might I suggest we do away with rank and call each other by our christian names. It would make life a lot easier, don't you think?'

'Agreed,' said Makowski, 'Now, I suppose we ought to be going. It strikes me we are sitting ducks here.'

He looked at Anders. 'There is nothing to keep us here now, is there, sir? If we want to be well east of the city by dawn, I think the sooner we move the better.'

'Very well,' said Anders. 'In that case it only remains for me to wish you luck and as trouble-free a journey as possible.'

Jacub Slowacki grabbed Albert's hand. 'I wish you one too, with all my heart. I am only sorry that you have not got all the gold, but at least if you get this consignment to America you will have done a wonderful job for Poland.' Albert felt Slowacki's hand shaking. 'You take the prayers of all this country with you, Mieszkowski; may God protect you and deliver you and Zaluski safely to Trieste.'

'Thank you, sir.'

The three men saluted and turned towards the trucks.

'I think it might be a good idea,' said Lech to the other two, 'If Andre takes the last truck and you and I, Albert, go in the first one. I suspect I know the route out of here better than you but by the time we reach Lublin I will have no idea where to go, and no doubt you will?'

'Like the back of my hand.'

'Good. Then let's do that. Is that okay with you, Andre?'

'Fine by me,' said Andre. 'But how do we keep in touch? Seventy trucks is one hell of a long column!'

'The front truck has the only short wave radio, but all the others have radio hand sets. They took some getting, I can tell you! If you have trouble, just shout!'

Andre started to move away. 'Okay. I will let you know when we are ready.'

Albert and Lech moved towards the front truck and got in beside the driver.

'Now all we have to do is pray,' said Albert nervously. 'It seems to me the first miracle will be if we get seventy trucks out of here all in one piece!'

Lech laughed. 'I shouldn't tell you this, but I don't believe in God! So I will just keep my fingers crossed!'

Albert gripped his companion's arm. 'Trust me to land up with the only atheist in Poland!'

Their laughter was interrupted by Andre's voice on the radio. 'I'm in the last truck and I've made sure all the engines in front of me are running. We are ready to go. Good luck!'

Albert wrote: *'The time to pray and cross my fingers had arrived. I felt exhilarated, not full of fear as I had done when leaving Bartek. I remember thinking that I must be becoming a hardened soldier!'*

For the first hour all went according to plan and as the driver weaved his way expertly round rubble, holes and people, Albert began to think that they might actually get out of Warsaw without too much trouble. Another half hour? With luck certainly. Then, if his memory served him right, it was about 160 kilometres to Lublin and if they were going to avoid the Luftwaffe, ideally they wanted to be very close to the town or, best of all, through it and on their way to Lvov by dawn.

160 kilometres. Could seventy trucks travel that distance in the eight hours to dawn? In normal circumstances the answer would be 'yes'. But with the roads choked by slow-moving people and a varied collection of vehicles, and some damage to the road as well, it became more problematic. He felt the sweat trickle down his face and knew that if he could not control his nerves he would soon be exhausted.

'Let's have that thermos of coffee,' he said to Lech. 'I need something to calm me down.'

Lech was just handing him the thermos when the truck abruptly stopped.

'Oh, oh!' exclaimed Lech, looking at the driver. 'It looks as if we have problems!'

The coffee forgotten, Albert pushed his face hard against the windscreen. 'What's the matter?'

'The bloody road is blocked,' said Lech. 'We can't get round that pile of rubble – just look at it!'

Albert felt his heart miss a beat. 'Christ, it looks as if a whole building has collapsed into the street!'

'A bloody big one at that!' said Lech. 'We will have to go back and try a different route.'

'How long will that take?'

'If we are lucky and find the route clear that I have in mind we should be out of Warsaw in another hour. If not . . . well, we will have to take a very long detour. You can make that two hours, then.'

Albert swallowed. 'I think I will just pray!'

Lech spoke into the hand set. 'Andre, are you receiving me?'

'Yes, I can hear you.'

'We are going to have to turn round. The road up here is blocked. I think we can all turn in the road, so let me come past first and then you try it. Has everyone heard that?'

The answer was a muddle of 'yes's.

'Blast these sets! That's the trouble when everyone tries to answer at once. We will just have to hope they all heard,' said Lech. He touched the driver on the shoulder. 'Okay, turn round and go past all the trucks.'

The driver completed the manoeuvre and drove slowly back down the way they had just come. As they drew level with Andre he waved.

Albert sat back. 'At least I counted them all. No one missing yet. My God, if we have to turn round seventy trucks many times our plans to be at Lublin by dawn will be in trouble.'

'I know, I know,' said Lech, his voice clearly showing his concern.

Albert grunted and looked out of the window at the destruction. *'I wondered what the world had come to,'* he wrote. *'How could one civilised nation wish so much death and damage on another. It made no sense. It was just utter folly or the work of a madman. I closed my eyes and rested my forehead on the glass – the coolness was so comforting – and wondered when the next crisis would arrive.'*

None came. And as Lech had forecast, an hour later they were passing through the last of the suburbs.

'Nearly made it,' he cried. He looked at Albert and then at the driver. 'Well done, that was not easy.'

Albert relaxed a bit and reached for the thermos. 'Thank God for that! Now, perhaps, I can enjoy a drink.'

Nevertheless, progress turned out to be frustratingly slow, not only because the dimmed headlights stopped them moving at a decent speed, but also because the road was still packed with people fleeing from the city. Albert had hoped that the tide would have ebbed a bit. The result was that they never moved above a fast walking pace and it soon became obvious that their goal of Lublin by dawn was unobtainable.

Then came the air strike.

The first they knew of it was when they saw the flashes from the plane's tracers coming towards them. The driver slammed on the brakes and ducked down below the dashboard. Seconds later Albert heard screaming coming from in front of the truck, and as the great mass of bodies panicked and fought to get off the road he could just make out one group bending over what he assumed was a body. It was chaos, and the trucks were jammed in the middle – perfect sitting targets. Sure enough, moments later a panicky voice came over the radio. 'Two trucks in front of me are on fire! Can you hear me, sir? Two trucks on fire!'

Lech spoke urgently. 'Yes, yes, man, I can hear you – identify yourself! Whereabouts in the column are you? You know your number, so quickly!'

'Thirty-four sir, thirty-four. My God, they have just blown up!'

The radio went dead. 'Christ, bang in the middle!' exclaimed Lech. 'I think it must be some of the fuel!'

Albert's bowels churned violently – the fear had returned!

The radio crackled. Lech cupped his hands over his ears – there was so much noise! 'Someone is trying to reach us.'

'Lech, Albert, are you receiving me?' It was Andre, his voice urgent but steady.

'Yes, yes, got you now!' said Lech.

'Thank God! Listen, I think it was a lone plane and it seems to have moved away now. Probably just came on us by accident and didn't realise what was beneath him. It passed over the entire column but luckily seems to have only hit numbers thirty-two and three. They were two of the fuel trucks – only one left now. I have sent a man up to see what we can do. But listen, I can't see any point in you and the front trucks hanging around only to get straafed again if any of the bastards return. Why don't you push on to Lublin? Then at least there is a chance of getting half our load away from here. I will try and move the two burning trucks and follow on later and will meet you the other side of the town.'

Albert glanced at Lech. 'It makes sense, and once we are through Lublin it won't hurt waiting for a bit.' He chewed at a nail and grabbed the hand-set. 'I don't like leaving you, Andre, but you are right, so we will go on and wait until midday tomorrow on the Lvov road just out of Lublin. Providing of course we get that far! If you haven't turned up by then try and get through on the radio and tell us where you are. If you are still some distance away we will move on to Mieszki Wielkie and wait for you there. Okay?'

'Yes, that's fine. Don't worry. It will take more than one bloody German to finish me!'

'I'm sure! See you outside Lublin then – best of luck!'

'And to you!'

'He will be in trouble if the Luftwaffe comes back,' said Lech quietly.

Albert shook his head. 'Christ, don't I know that!' There was a moment's silence in the cab before he continued. 'But no good dwelling on it! If we are going to move, let's get going. See if you can reach the other drivers. I suspect most of them are out of their trucks. If so, I will run back down the road and tell them what we are going to do. When I reach the wrecked trucks I will get into the one in front of them and radio through to you. No point in wasting time waiting for me to come back when you know the way to Lublin.'

Lech spoke once again into the radio. 'Can any drivers hear me?'

There was no answer and he repeated the question. Only two replied.

'Forget it!' said Albert, 'It's wasting valuable time. I'm off. Will contact you when I'm ready.'

Lech raised a hand as Albert jumped out of the lorry and set off at a run down the road.

It was not as easy an exercise as he had imagined it would be for the sides of the road were cluttered with people all either trying to find belongings that they had dropped in their panic or calling out for friends or relatives from whom they had got separated. And he didn't know if all the drivers were on the same side of the road. 'If only it was bloody daylight,' he thought. By the time he reached the third truck he realised he had set himself an impossible task. He had to think of something quickly. He reached up and, pulling himself into the cab, banged his hand hard down on the horn. 'Come on, come on!' he thought. Suddenly a very agitated driver was beside him. It had worked!

'What the bloody hell . . .!' He swung a torch onto Albert and saw the uniform. 'Oh, sorry sir! I thought . . .'

Albert pushed the torch away. 'Forget it! No time for apologies! We must move quickly. As you probably know, two trucks have been hit. So Captain Makowski and I have decided there is little point in all of us hanging around here waiting for another attack. We have decided to move on with all the trucks in front of the wrecked ones. The problem is, we can't raise the drivers. So I decided to run down the road to tell them. But Christ, what hope have I got! It's dark, the road is blocked by all these damned people, and I haven't got a clue where everyone is. Do you think sounding the horns would work?'

'Why not, sir, it worked for me.'

'Right! You keep hold of your radio and you will hear me contact Captain Makowski when we are ready to move.'

The driver nodded as Albert lowered himself back onto the road and started pushing his way towards the next truck.

It worked a treat! Some came quicker than others but in half an hour he was at the burning wreckage and all the drivers in front of him were at their wheels.

'I'm coming with you,' he told the last man. 'First I must contact Captain Zaluski in the rear truck. Call him up, will you?'

The driver nodded. 'Captain Zaluski, can you hear me?' He repeated the question several times. 'No luck, sir, I can't raise him.'

Damn! Then I will have to talk to the driver on the other side of the wreckage. Do you know if anyone survived from the two fuel trucks?'

'I doubt it sir – but I can't say definitely. There was a blinding flash and then a few minutes later whoosh! The whole sky seemed to explode!'

'Okay. Just get your engine started.'

Albert walked round the burning vehicles – the heat was intense. It seemed to him impossible that anyone could have got out alive. He shuddered and looked away. Poor bastards!

He found the next driver sitting slumped in his cab with the door open. Albert could see him clearly in the light from the fire. He looked very young and was shaking with shock.

Albert reached up and shook his shoulder.

'Hey! Come on. There's work to be done.'

The young man jumped and shook his head. 'They just blew up! Bang! Then they were engulfed in flames! The poor sods didn't stand a chance!'

Albert grabbed his wrist. 'I know, I know. But you have got things to do. Do you understand?'

'Yes, yes, I suppose so.'

'Christ, he's crying!' thought Albert.

He let go of the wrist and slapped the man's face hard. 'No bloody "suppose so" soldier, your life depends on it. You must do as I say!'

Albert watched the young man rub his cheek. Had he got through to him?

'I'm all right now, sir, really I am. It was just . . .' His voice trailed off.

'Good. Now listen. Captain Makowski and I are taking on the trucks in front of you to Lublin. You must wait here until another officer makes contact with you. He is coming up from the rear of the column and should be here soon. Make sure to tell him that you have spoken to me. Is that clear?'

'Yes sir. But who will that be?'

'You won't know him – there was no time in Warsaw for us to make ourselves known to everyone – but his name is Captain Andre Zaluski. Now keep a hold of yourself and be patient. I promise you he will come.'

There was no more time to waste – he couldn't be nursemaid as well as everything else. He turned away and ran past the burning vehicles back to the truck and jumped into the cab. He reached for the radio. 'Lech, Lech. Are you there?'

'Receiving you clearly, Albert. All okay?'

'Yes, after a little difficulty. It's fine now and all our trucks will be able to hear you. So let's get moving!'

Lech tapped his driver on the shoulder. 'Foot down, young man, and let's hope we have seen the last of the Luftwaffe.'

'I felt a real bastard leaving Andre,' wrote Albert. *'But he was right. It was no good us all sitting there to be shot at. As the truck moved forward I wondered if I would ever see my friend again.'*

Chapter 5

Dawn on 8 September saw them well short of their target in spite of no further air attacks. The problem was that the tide of people had not lessened and much as Lech wanted to push on it would have been impossible without risking the lives of those who trudged in front of them. It had been a frustrating time and soon after they had continued their journey Albert began to chivvy him from behind until he had lost his temper.

'For God's sake, man, shut up! We have a human wall in front of us and, gold or not, I refuse to run any of them down. However, if you think you can do better then get your arse up here and show me how!'

There had been no more adverse remarks.

Now, as the first rays of the sun glinted on the truck windows, it became all too apparent how desperately slow their progress had been that night. Of the 160 kilometres that Albert had reckoned they would have to travel to reach Lublin by dawn they had only managed 60. Lech wondered if they were far enough on to avoid the interests of the Luftwaffe.

As if in answer to his thoughts he heard Albert calling him up on the radio. 'Lech, Lech, can you hear me?'

'Loud and clear. Are you thinking what I am?'

'About the Luftwaffe?'

'Yes.'

'Well, we can only hope he had a late night and is not too keen to start early this morning! What's the road like now?'

Lech smiled. He could almost hear Albert controlling his impatience. 'Still a lot of people but I should say a little clearer.' He glanced at the speedometer. 'As no doubt you will have noticed, we have managed to increase our speed a bit.'

'I know, but at 25 kilometres per hour we will be lucky to be through Lublin by this evening.'

'Correct, but does that matter so much if we are not going to be shot at by the Luftwaffe? In fact, it might be to our advantage. With any luck Andre will have found the road clearer behind us and then we won't have so long to wait once we reach Lublin.'

Albert sounded thoroughly depressed when he replied. 'I'm not sure I give him much of a chance. I have a nasty feeling he will have been attacked again.'

Lech thought for a moment before replying, 'Well, I hope to God you're wrong! I'm sure you are aware that if he doesn't get through we have no provisions or spare fuel.'

'For Christ sake, don't remind me! I know. However, we should have enough fuel to get to Lublin. If the worst happens we should be able to get fuel there. If not, we are finished.'

Albert's voice trailed off and Lech almost felt sorry for him. What a change from life in Paris!

'Look,' he replied. 'Panicking will do us no good. Let's stop for a few minutes – take a breather and let everyone stretch their legs and have a drink if their thermoses are not already empty. It won't delay us that much. I am sure everything will work out, and if it doesn't, then, too bad – there is nothing we can do about it.'

'Okay, you stop when you are ready.'

Lech put down the hand set and banged a fist hard down on the seat. He had deliberately wanted to sound relaxed to Albert but in fact he was a very worried man inside. Not least because he knew they had been in too much of a hurry to get away from the rest of the convoy. They should never have left without taking some spare fuel or provisions. It could prove a fatal mistake.

He touched the driver's arm. 'We will stop here for ten minutes. Time to stretch the legs and have a warm drink. I will pass the order down the radio.'

In fact, once they started again, Lady Luck rode with them and after two hours they were able to increase their speed a little more as the choking masses seemed to thin out. Lech wasn't quite sure why, but the increased number of groups huddled by the side of the road seemed to explain it. Exhaustion and the need for a meal of some sorts seemed to be the logical answer. Whatever the cause, for the first time since they had set out from Warsaw, he could see the road for more than a few metres in front of him and by one o'clock they were on the outskirts of Lublin.

Immediately, he gave the order for the trucks to stop and contacted Albert.

'I have been thinking it might be wiser for us to wait for Andre on this side of the town. If we drive through and he fails to turn up we will only have to retrace our steps to try and find food and fuel in the town.'

There was a grunt down the line. 'How long should we give him?'

Lech reflected that Albert was supposed to be making the decisions. He bit back a sarcastic comment, mainly because it was in his nature to be a leader and he enjoyed being in command. If that was what Albert wanted, then he would oblige.

'I would suggest that we give him until five o'clock. We are exposed here, I know, but as we have seen no enemy activity in the air so far I don't see why we should now.'

'Okay, but isn't five a bit late if we have got to try and find fuel?'

'I don't think so, and besides, we all need a rest. Post some lookouts and make sure everyone else gets some sleep. I know that might not be easy on empty stomachs but we were getting used to that in Warsaw.'

'Very well.'

Albert made sure that everyone had heard the order before getting out of the truck. He could have done with some food but he wasn't going to let Lech know that. He had shown him one weakness already – he had no intention of revealing another. He stretched – he was so tired – he could have done with some sleep, but it was his job to stay awake. He sat down on the verge and put his head in his hands – he would just close his eyes for a minute . . .

He was woken by someone vigorously shaking his shoulder.

'Sir! Sir!'

He stared blankly up at the soldier. Where was he? God, had he fallen asleep? His mind was numb.

'Sir, the trucks, I think I can see the trucks!'

Albert shook his head. The trucks? They were all here! What was the stupid man talking about? He got shakily to his feet. 'What trucks?'

With exasperation showing in his voice the soldier tried again. 'You know sir – the rest of the convoy – the trucks we left behind last night.'

Albert slapped his forehead with the palm of his hand. Oh my God! Andre! Could it really be that he had got through? He was alert now – cursing his addled brain.

He grabbed the soldier's arm. 'Sorry! Let's go and see.'

They ran past the truck onto a small rise just off the road. It was straight for at least a mile. The soldier pointed and offered his field glasses.

'I don't need those – I can see the bloody trucks!' It had to be Andre. He glanced at his watch – 2.00 p.m. They must have done bloody well!

He turned to the soldier, trying to speak calmly. 'I'm sure it's them! Get back to the radio and tell Captain Makowski and then stay with the radio in case Captain Zaluski tries to make contact. I will stay here and make sure it's not Germans.'

As soon as the soldier had gone Albert was filled with doubt. Why hadn't Andre tried to make contact? He was close enough. Was it a trap? Had the trucks been captured and now the Germans were coming on in the hope that they would find the rest of the gold? Why, oh why, didn't Andre make radio contact! Perhaps he should run back and try. But that had not been the agreed procedure when they had parted. If it was Germans it was better to keep radio silence and with luck he would see something that would give the game away before they got too close. How long should he wait? Christ, the agony of not knowing!

'Sir!'

Albert jumped and looked round at the soldier. 'Yes?'

'I have them on the radio! It's them, sir.'

He grabbed the set out of the soldier's hand. 'Andre! It's Albert here. Can you hear me?'

'My God, you sound wonderful!' came back the reply. 'Where are you?'

'Can you see the end of the road?'

'Yes, I think I can just see it turn to the left. Is that right?'

Albert choked back the tears. 'Yes, yes. Well, that's where we are!' He almost cried down the radio, 'Did you hear that, Lech?'

'I did, and I will be with you as quickly as I can.'

Albert sat back in the cab, feeling quite weak. *'I don't think I have ever felt so relieved,'* he wrote. *'Until that moment I hadn't realised how much he meant to me.'*

He was still thinking of his friend as Lech climbed in beside him. He jumped as Lech thumped his shoulder. 'They won't be long now!'

He smiled and wiped away his tears. 'My God, Lech, I shall be glad to see him!'

Ten minutes later he and Andre were hugging each other.

'I thought I had seen the last of you!' said Albert as he stood back, shaking his head. 'I had persuaded myself that you had been killed.'

Andre, almost out on his feet and covered in grime from head to foot, managed a smile. 'Well, that was bloody pessimistic, if you don't mind my saying so! In fact it was all very easy really.' He grimaced. 'Once the fires had died down we had to retrieve what was left of the two drivers.

Luckily no one was travelling in the back with the fuel. Then we just drove over the wreckage. All we suffered was one blown tyre.'

'No more Luftwaffe?' asked Lech.

'Not a sign. Thank God. For our progress was agonisingly slow, which I assume yours must have been?'

'Bloody awful,' said Albert. 'It did get better a few hours ago, and we could have got further, but we decided to wait here in case you didn't arrive and we had to try and find fuel in the town.'

Lech turned to Andre. 'We should never have gone off without some fuel. However, that's history now. We are all bloody glad to see you. What say we give the men some food and bury our dead before moving on? This looks as good a place as any.'

'That sounds a good idea. I will get a detail to dig the graves.'

It took them an hour, an hour in which most of the men experienced for the first time the disturbing task of burying comrades in a strange field far from their homes. Even the sight of much-needed food and a hot drink failed to raise their spirits, and it was a quiet and reflective band of men that returned to their trucks and drove on to Lublin.

The town had escaped the heavy bombing suffered by Warsaw; Albert's fear that the bridge over the river Bystrzyca might have been destroyed proved unfounded and the convoy was able to proceed along the almost deserted streets unhindered. To Albert, who knew the town well, it was a strange feeling rumbling past the relatively new factories with their gates closed and not a soul in sight and the centre as quiet as if it was three o'clock on a cold winter's morning. He wondered where on earth everybody had got to.

By mid-afternoon they were clear of the town and facing the drive to Lvov some 200 kilometres away.

'You're on your own now,' said Lech to Albert who had rejoined him in the front truck. 'I have never been further than Lublin.'

'Then feast your eyes on some of the best scenery in Poland,' said Albert as he tried to make himself comfortable in the cramped confines of the cab.

'I was still desperately tired,' he wrote, *'But so keyed up that I knew there was no danger of falling asleep again. After all, I was going home, something that a few days ago I had given up hope of ever doing again.'*

They reached Lvov early on the morning of 10 September and from there it was only an hour's drive to Mieszki Wielkie.

The first thing Albert saw through the trees was the roof of the house glinting in the September sun. *'I'm crying even now as I write although it is weeks later. I was overcome with emotion – I was home. My feeling of joy was indescribable.'*

As the trucks wound their way up the long tree-lined drive he looked out of the window with mounting excitement. He saw several familiar faces staring at the convoy with an element of fear obvious in their eyes and he leant out of the cab shouting to them that all was well. By the time they drew up in front of the house quite a crowd was running along behind the convoy, all eager to see what the young Mieszkowski was doing bringing so many trucks to Mieszki Wielkie.

Alerted by the noise, his father had come running out of the house and was standing on the drive looking in amazement at the long line of trucks when he saw his son jump out of the leading vehicle and run towards him.

'Albert! Dear God, how wonderful to see you!' His mouth fell open in surprise.

'I was tingling with excitement as we embraced,' wrote Albert. *'I felt as if I wanted to explode, so happy was I to see him. I somehow managed to tell him I would explain everything, before asking him if mother and Barbara were all right.'*

'Yes, yes, fine,' Jacek choked out, before becoming speechless. In front of him stood his son whom he had resigned himself to never seeing again. It was asking too much even for a man of such rigorous upbringing to stay calm and unmoved.

He kissed Albert on both cheeks. 'You are the best thing I have ever seen in my life! Just wait until your mother and sister see you! And your sister will have a surprise for you as well. But more of that later – tell me, boy, what brings you here with all these trucks? At first, some of the men here thought you were the Germans arriving!'

Albert looked round and saw Lech and Andre coming towards him. 'Let me introduce you first to my brother officers. Although I am sure you will remember Andre Zaluski.'

Jacek shook his head. 'The Zaluski who took my Hispano-Suiza for a drive when I wasn't looking?'

'The very one!' laughed Albert as Andre and Lech stopped beside him.

'Hello, sir,' said Andre, holding out a hand. 'I expect you hoped that you had seen the last of me!'

Jacek shook his hand vigorously. 'Never! I always liked you. I felt a man as bold as you was good for my son. Besides, I think my drive with you later evened things out, eh?'

Andre laughed as he remembered the terrifying drive along the tracks of Mieszki Wielkie in the Hispano-Suiza that he had been subjected to as a punishment for driving the car without permission. 'Now I will show you how to really drive!' Jacek had said. My God, he had certainly done that!

'I was only talking about it the other day to Albert, sir. How could I ever forget!'

Albert interrupted them. 'And this, father, is Captain Lech Makowski.'

Lech smiled and shook Jacek's hand. 'Albert has told me a lot about you, sir, in the last few days.'

'Not all bad, I hope,' laughed Jacek.

'Far from it, sir.'

'Good, good. And now that the introductions are complete perhaps you can tell me what this is all about?'

'Tell him, Albert,' said Lech.

'I think, father, that you may find this hard to believe, but in these trucks is one hundred and fifty million dollars of gold bullion from the State Bank in Warsaw. It is our job to try and get it through to Trieste where, if all goes well, a British destroyer will take it to America.'

'Good God!' said Jacek.

'That's actually exactly what Andre and I said when we were told the plan by our Ambassador in Paris.'

Recovering quickly from the shock, Jacek said, 'That doesn't explain why you got the job or why you are here?'

'No. The answer to that is still mystifying me a little. We were told that my diplomatic status and knowledge of this region might help us get through to Trieste and Andre knows the Carpathians well from his climbing holidays. I also think the army commanders in Warsaw felt they could not spare any officers. The second part of your question is simple. You see, father, the original plan was for Andre and I to proceed first to our respective estates and recruit drivers and then go to Warsaw. However, the Germans moved faster than anyone imagined and cut off Andre's route to his estate and it became obvious that we could not delay getting the gold out of Warsaw. As it is, believe it or not, this is only half of it! The rest is still in Warsaw.'

Jacek blew out his cheeks. 'Good heavens!'

Albert continued. 'However, as our only safe route out of Poland is from the east and as we couldn't take as big an escort as we would have liked out of Warsaw, and because we are desperately short of rifles, we thought we would come here on our way and still try and recruit some help and perhaps find men with rifles. If successful, we could then send some of the regular soldiers back to Warsaw.'

Jacek nodded his head. 'I see. It seems to me, however, you are pitifully armed to defend such a valuable cargo.'

'I agree. We can only hope the Germans won't get as far as the Tatras for a little longer.'

Jacek shook his head at his son. 'Yes, the Tatras. My God, Albert, you have chosen a hard route!'

'I know. However it is our only hope. We will cross by the road that goes to Mukacevo. September shouldn't be too bad. As I said, Andre knows the mountains well.'

Jacek looked at the three young men in front of him. 'Knowing the mountains from climbing is one thing. To drive all these trucks through a pass is another matter altogether. Even in September the Tatras can be wicked. I am sure I don't need to tell you that they can be very cruel. You will need all your skills and much luck.'

Albert nodded. 'I know, father, I know. But we have half the wealth of Poland with us and it must be saved for the future of this country.'

Jacek looked at his son sadly. 'Do you think it has a future?'

'I do, father – I have to.'

Jacek did not press the point. 'Very well, then, I wish every one of you the best of luck. Now, how many men have you got? Can we get them all into the house?'

Albert answered. 'Eighty-eight. We started with ninety, but lost two men and two fuel trucks on the way to a Luftwaffe attack. Surely you and mother don't want them all in the house? I'm sure they will be quite happy in some of the barns.'

'No question about it,' said Jacek. 'Of course they must billet in the house and I will send a few men to get food from the villages. Apart from meat, I doubt if we have enough here.'

'Thank you, father. I am sure they will be very grateful.'

'How long do you plan to stay?'

'As short a time as possible, I'm afraid. No more than two days. We have some repairs to do as well as trying to recruit men.'

'I see,' said Jacek. 'Well, I hope you can find the men – that might not be as easy as you think. Nor will finding a good supply of fuel. Although I think I may be able to help there. More of that later. Now, how about getting your men sorted out. I would suggest they camp down in the ballroom and the big hall?'

'That sounds fine,' said Albert. 'We will organise . . .'

He never finished his sentence. For at that moment, Barbara came running out of the house. 'Albert! Oh, dear God, is it really you!'

She ran into his arms, tears streaming down her face.

Andre and Lech looked at each other and moved off back to the trucks to organise the men. They had no desire to intrude on Albert's homecoming.

Wiping away her tears, Barbara grabbed her brother's arm. 'Come on, come on, you must see mother, and have I got some news for you!'

For a second he resisted, thinking that he should join Andre and Lech, but the temptation was too strong and he allowed himself to be led into the hall where he stopped in surprise.

'The portraits? Where have they all gone?'

Barbara looked round the empty walls. 'Father decided to send the most valuable pictures and furniture to the Embassy in Paris. He sent them by road a week ago.'

'Then I fear they may never reach their destination, as I expect he sent them west and the Germans have all but overrun that part of the country, and they are certain to have intercepted any traffic trying to get across the border. I would say some fat murderous German is by now the proud owner of much of our heritage.'

'Oh Albert! That will break his heart!'

'Then we won't tell him or mother. Do you agree?'

Barbara was on the verge of tears again. 'Yes. It would be the kindest thing to do. Though if we get through to Paris he is bound to find out then.'

'So he is going to leave?'

'Yes. He and mother are resigned to it now. He has heard terrible stories of what the Germans are doing to our countrymen.'

Albert sighed with relief. He had harboured the feeling that his father would refuse to go.

'Well, I'm bloody glad he has seen sense. Now, before I see mother, tell us this piece of news.'

'I'm going to marry Kasimir.'

'My God, sister, that was quick!'

'I know. But I love him, Albert – he's so kind and very good-looking. I'm sorry he is not here to meet you, but unfortunately, like everyone else, he is rather busy at the moment.'

She laughed and squeezed her brother's hand. She so wanted his approval.

'You're so young.'

Her eyes flashed angrily. 'Not you as well, Albert! That's all mother says. Father says nothing so I know he disapproves. Neither have said "no", I'm glad to say. Although I'm sure this is only because of the crisis.'

'Well, if they have agreed at all he must be nice and I wish you all the luck in the world,' said Albert. 'When do you plan to marry?'

'Just as soon as we can. I hope that Kasimir will be here next week. So then, if possible. Our time together could be very short. Will you be able to stay?'

'I'm afraid not – we should be gone in two days. But don't worry, I will be thinking of you.' He pulled her to him and kissed her lovingly. 'I'm really pleased for you, little sister – I really am.'

'Oh Albert, I can't tell you how happy that makes me feel. Now you'd better go and see mother. No doubt she will tell you what an impetuous girl I am! I told her it was her own fault for shutting me away all those years in that awful convent!'

Albert shook his head. 'You haven't changed! Now where is she?'

'In the drawing room.'

Krystina was sitting in her favourite chair in an almost empty room and as Albert hurried towards her he thought she looked lost and afraid in the vast room now shorn of most of its furniture and pictures.

'Mother!'

She held out her arms. 'Albert! Darling Albert, I heard it was you! But to tell you the truth I was too frightened to come and see if it was really true, for your father had almost persuaded me you were dead. I kept saying nothing could have happened to you in Paris, but when your calls stopped abruptly he believed you had come back to Poland to fight. It looks as if he was right!'

'Not quite. We are here because we have been given a particular job. I will tell you more later. And I'm sorry that I didn't get through to you to tell you what was happening, but when we were told to move there wasn't time.'

Krystina smiled. 'I understand. You look terribly tired. Come and sit down here on the floor and tell me everything that has happened to you since you last left.'

He lowered himself to the floor and, laying his head on her knees, he told her everything, and as he talked she kept running her long manicured fingers through his filthy hair and her touch brought brutally home to him that, independent as he had become, he still needed her, and that his life would be shattered if he lost her in the boiling cauldron that his country had become.

When he had finished she said nothing for a few minutes, content to stroke his hair in silence. Eventually she asked, 'What do you think of Barbara's piece of news?'

'I'm pleased for her, mother, though surprised by the speed.'

'Us too.Though he seems kind enough. To tell you the truth, your father would have said "no", but times are not normal, are they? So we can only pray it works out and that above all the Lord allows them to have a life together.'

Albert looked up at his mother. 'I think that was very generous of him. How is he anyway?'

Krystina shrugged. 'Oh, you know your father. Convinced that I will melt away with worry. He has been so loving that I almost feel claustrophobic. I don't mean that unkindly, – but if only he would allow me to share his worries. Together it would be so much easier. As it is, we both pretend to each other. He won't change, I know. So I just pray every now and then that God will not forget us completely in this complicated world he seems to have concocted.'

Albert stroked her knee and closed his eyes. *'I desperately needed a few minutes alone with her,'* he wrote.

Their hopes of being away from Mieszki Wielkie within two days were dashed by three aggravating problems.

Valuable time was wasted scouring the villages for recruits that were just not forthcoming – or at least none that Jacek thought reliable, and so in the end they reached the conclusion that rather than take men who might only be a burden to them, they would have to ignore their orders and keep all the soldiers they had brought out of Warsaw. Given the chaotic state of the Polish army, Albert felt it was unlikely that they would ever have to justify their decision in front of General Anders anyway.

Then there was the lack of fuel. They needed to replace the stock they had lost on the two trucks, as well as a bit more for any emergencies, and in spite of Jacek's hard work he just could not put his hands on a supply big enough to satisfy their demands.

Albert reckoned that, barring any unforeseen circumstances, they probably had enough to get them to Budapest, but felt it was worth hanging on a little longer in the hope that his father might find the elusive supply that would take away all their worries.

Finally there were the trucks. All of them were old and past their best and the slow drive from Warsaw had severely tested one or two gearboxes as well as showing up dozens of minor faults that if ignored could lead to mechanical breakdowns at the most inopportune moment. Andre reckoned that it would be sheer folly to try and cross the Tatras until some of the faults had been repaired.

So, as each morning broke, they found they had to delay their departure yet again. Finally, on the afternoon of 14 September when they heard on the radio that Warsaw had been encircled, it was clear that they stayed at Mieszki Wielkie at their peril. They would just have to make the best of what they had already achieved.

Nevertheless they did not get away for another forty-eight hours, as two gearboxes were proving difficult to repair, and although they could afford to abandon one truck and transfer the gold, to leave two was out of the question. So they worked frantically on the damage to one gearbox by using parts from the truck they had decided to abandon. After that, any minor faults still unfinished had to be forgotten and the fuel situation accepted, for they all felt that the time had come to throw caution to the wind – if they delayed further, their one remaining escape route could easily be found blocked.

So on the evening of 16 September Albert ordered the convoy to be ready by dawn the next day.

It was a perfect autumn morning as Albert climbed into the leading truck. It had been agreed the night before that this time he and Andre would head the convoy and Lech would bring up the rear. To give themselves more room for their maps, rifles, and radio Albert had decided that they would dispense with their driver.

He gripped the wheel and looked across at Andre. 'Ready?'

'As much as I ever will be!' He smiled and patted his friend's shoulder. He knew the agony that Albert was suffering at the thought of leaving his family behind and the very real possibility that he would never see his home again. He had already gone through a similar type of hell.

'Are they still there?' asked Albert.

Andre twisted in his seat and leaned out of the window. Jacek had an arm round each of the two women standing beside him.

'Yes.'

'God! Do they have to watch us leave!'

Albert pulled violently at the starter and shuddered as the engine fired.

'Hang on!' cried Andre, 'Your father is waving frantically.'

Albert felt himself go cold all over. *'I knew my father wouldn't stop me unless it was urgent,'* he wrote. *'For our separation was as painful to him as to me. Reluctantly I pulled down my window.'*

'Trouble,' he said quietly. 'Russia invaded us about two hours ago!'

'Oh my God!'

'You must move fast, boy! You have no time to waste!'

'What about you?'

'Don't worry about us. We will get away, I promise. Now get on! For God sake, put your foot down!'

Without another glance at his father, Albert wound up the window and looked at Andre. 'Christ! That is all we need!'

He released the brake and thumped the truck into gear, pressing his foot down on the accelerator. What a time to have to leave his family. He knew he could not stay to see that they got away safely, but, oh God, the pain was awful. He could hardly see through his tears as he guided the truck down the drive and away from the house.

The time he had been able to spend alone with his family had been lamentably small. Whenever he had been able to grab the odd moment he'd had to deal with a near-hysterical mother or a weeping sister, who every day expected Kasimir to appear, and when he did not, shut herself in her room in the early evening and did not come out again until the next morning. It had done nothing to allay his distress. If it had not been for his father his stay would have been almost intolerable. He had been wonderful, relishing helping his son to prepare for the arduous and risky journey ahead and putting his heart into everything he did. At times Albert wished that he could come with them on the journey.

He hit the main road, praying that his father would leave Mieszki Wielkie as soon as possible. Any delay now would be endangering his family and he felt sure that was the last thing his father would willingly do. Anyway, he had no other choice but to believe that. For to doubt him would cause him untold misery.

He felt a touch on his jacket and looked across at Andre.

'What?'

'Lech says, could you go a little slower?'

He looked at the speedometer. He hadn't realised that the damn truck could go so fast! He had been in a world of his own.

'Tell him I'm sorry,' and he eased back his foot.

They reached Lvov in under an hour and as he pointed the truck south towards the mountains, Albert took one hand off the wheel and gestured towards them.

'Only 216 kilometres to Mukacevo,' he said. 'It will be a piece of cake!'

Chapter 6

The most severe climate in the whole of Poland is in the Tatra mountains. The winters are long and the spring and summer seem all too short. There is a thick covering of snow for more than two hundred days of the year and it was into this unfriendly environment that Albert led the convoy, well aware that they were inadequately equipped to stand the cold, even in September, if they were forced to stop for too long. They lacked warm clothes and any means of stopping the radiators from freezing. If that wasn't enough to worry about, he had the Russians behind him and was not sure that the trucks would be able to negotiate the narrow pass to which they were heading. However, Andre had convinced him and Lech that if they had to cross the Tatras he had chosen the only route that gave them a semblance of a chance.

The road from Lvov stretched out in front of them and, for a change, not a refugee or another vehicle was in sight. With nothing to hinder it the convoy made good time, and by five that evening they were eating up the kilometres at a satisfactory speed and nearing the foothills of the Tatras.

'I think we should stop here for the night,' suggested Andre, bent over the map. 'We don't want to reach the pass in the dark and if we get too high frost may become a risk.'

Albert nodded. 'I think you are right. The Russians can't have got this far yet. Radio through to Lech and tell him. We can pull off to the side of the road. After we have eaten we must post guards at the front and rear of the convoy just in case we have any unwanted visitors.'

He braked to a halt, stretched, and waited for Andre to stop talking to Lech before jumping out of the cab. He shivered – already the evening chill was setting in. It would be cold higher up.

Andre joined him with a flask. 'Here, have a warm drink and then we will make our way back to Lech. He is moving up to the provision trucks and will wait for us there.'

Once they had eaten and fixed a sentry roster there was nothing else to do but settle down in their cabs and wait for dawn. By eleven o'clock the cold was already eating into their bones, and, if you wanted to keep warm, sleep was not the answer. Like the majority of their men Andre and Albert spent the remaining hours till dawn either taking brisk walks up and down the road or huddled together in the cab drinking coffee.

By dawn they were all cold and tired, and their morale took a nosedive when they saw that the sunshine of the day before had been replaced by a thick impenetrable fog. Albert wrote, *'I quickly decided that it would be suicide to try and move forward in such conditions and when I put it to the other two they agreed.'*

With no sun the temperature was reluctant to climb and the men sat huddled round their trucks shivering, and by midday, when the weather had not improved, Albert began to grow nervous.

'What do you think?' he asked Andre, as they walked their now familiar route up and down the convoy.

'I doubt if it will clear today. For the men's sake, perhaps we ought to risk moving on. After all, we know there is little if any traffic in front of us and if we go very slowly I expect we will see the verges of the road. Actually, do we have a choice? If we stay here all day we will be cold before dusk arrives and I don't think anyone relishes another night like the last one.'

Albert rubbed his forehead. 'I know. But have we got a chance of getting through the pass before dark? If not, we are just substituting a cold spot for an even colder one and if we have an accident it just means it is more likely that the Russians might catch up with us. Unless you can assure me that we can pass the highest point safely before we have to stop I think it is better to remain here and try again tomorrow.'

'Okay, point taken,' said Andre. 'Let's go and ask Lech what he thinks.'

Lech never hesitated. 'Remain here. Tomorrow whatever happens we must move on.'

Albert once again admired his decisiveness. 'Very well, let's do that. Better go and break the news to the men.'

No one was happy about the decision but all accepted it was the wisest, and settled down to prepare for another cold and uncomfortable night, encouraged by the knowledge that at least they knew they would move on the next day whatever the conditions.

At about 1 o'clock a.m. someone spotted a star. Within minutes the whole convoy was buzzing.

'I think it's cleared,' said Andre.

'Then pray like hell that it doesn't come back before we can move,' replied Albert through chattering teeth.

No one even tried to sleep for the few hours remaining till dawn, for everyone was impatient to be away, and as the sky lightened in the east, they eased their stiffened limbs out of their trucks and hurried to the fire that Lech had kept burning all night to eat their second breakfast of stale sandwiches washed down with much needed hot cups of coffee. The atmosphere was very different to the morning before, because the fog had not come down again, and as the sun rose over the mountains they knew their idleness was over.

Nevertheless the cold had taken its toll, and their minds and reactions were not as sharp as they might have been, which caused the accident three hours later that once again brought the convoy to a halt.

On either side of the road were deep gulleys to take the water from the melting snow coming down from the mountains, and it was while negotiating a sharp bend that the driver of the third truck lost his grip on his steering wheel. Before he could correct the fault, the truck had rolled into the gulley and turned on its side. That would not have been disastrous as the road was still clear, but the driver following had to take evasive action, and in his hurry swung his wheel too hard to the right. The truck skidded across the road, turned almost a full circle and crashed into the next truck coming round the corner.

Immediately Albert's radio went mad. 'Christ, Andre, what are they all shouting?'

Andre had gone very white. 'Seems there has been an accident behind us.'

Albert slammed on his brakes. 'Jesus, no!'

He looked at Andre in disbelief before jumping down onto the road and waiting for his friend to join him. Sounding thoroughly dispirited he said, 'Better go and see what's happened, I suppose.'

It was bad. Very bad. One truck was on its side and two had their bonnets locked together, completely blocking the road.

'It's as clear to me now as it was then,' wrote Albert. *'My heart sank to my boots as I surveyed the scene, and I wondered if we would ever get out of the mess.'*

'Not very good sir!' said a soldier as Albert and Andre arrived.

Albert swore and put his head in his hand. Now what the hell were they going to do!

In fact, as Lech said when he arrived, there was only one answer. The truck off the road had to be unloaded and the bullion distributed around the remaining trucks. They hadn't the time or the equipment to right it and get it back on the road. The other two had to be dragged apart. Only then could it be assessed if they would be drivable again. 'Otherwise,' he said with a wry grin, 'We might as well all sit down here and wait for the Germans, or their comrades the Russians!'

They had no suitable equipment even for prising two vehicles apart, and on closer inspection they were not going to free them with their bare hands. Albert cursed loudly that they hadn't thought of bringing a chain, and the looks that passed between the three men said it all.

Lech was the first to break the silence. 'We can take some of the rope that is holding the boxes down in the trucks and see if we can pull them apart. We will soon find out if the rope is strong enough. And while some of us are doing that, I suggest we organise a detail to shift the gold from the demobilised truck.'

With the orders given and Andre agreeing to take charge of moving the gold, Albert and Lech plus a dozen men collected four ropes and plaited them together to make two stronger lengths. Even so, Lech looked at the finished pieces with doubt. 'Well, I don't know – I wouldn't put much money on them holding!'

'You're a cheerful bugger!' said Albert. 'Anyway, only one way to find out.'

Albert drove his truck forward out of the way, and they manoeuvred the truck behind him close to the back of one of the entangled vehicles and attached the two ropes to the rear axle.

'Right,' said Lech to the driver, 'Ease yourself forward slowly.'

Albert saw one of the bumpers move slightly, but just as he thought they were going to succeed on the first attempt the ropes broke.

'Damn!' he cried. 'So bloody nearly!'

They replaited the ropes and tried again – and again – and again. More rope was used, more valuable daylight lost. Yet each time a little bit more of the bumpers were prised apart.

'We're going to win!' said Lech.

'Maybe,' said Albert, 'Although not before we have lost another day.'

And win they did, just before dusk, and in spite of losing more valuable time, Albert was surprised at the feeling of elation as he watched the two vehicles drawn apart. However, it was too late for them to contemplate moving on, and they were condemned to another cold night with still the pass and the border – a seemingly unreachable goal.

'Dear God,' said Albert to Lech as he helped him build a fire, 'I thought we would be over the Tatras by now and well on our way to Budapest.'

'Lech knew I was feeling the strain,' wrote Albert, *'He did his best to cheer me up. Even said our luck would change and by tomorrow evening we would be through the pass and well on the way to Budapest. I remember only too well that I didn't believe him.'*

They moved on at four o'clock the next morning, fearful that the Russians might be very close. Or could it be the Germans? For all they knew Poland had surrendered. It was an uneasy feeling, being out of touch.

Of one thing they were certain, speed was of the utmost importance. Risks would have to be taken now regardless of the weather. The border was not far, but if they continued at their present rate could take days to reach! They just had to pray that they made no more mistakes!

Andre saw them as they topped the rise and started to go down a hill. He stared in amazement through the windscreen. He saw several more. Oh my God! Had Albert seen them?

He was grabbing at his friend's sleeve just as the first burst of automatic fire shattered the glass in front of him and blew off half his head.

'I still find it hard to believe,' wrote Albert. *'I remember looking at all the blood and losing control of the truck. I think I was screaming – I can't be sure. I vaguely remember hurtling down the road out of control – but then perhaps that is what I was told. I remember nothing more. But piecing it together as I lay in a hospital in Budapest a few weeks later I must have been thrown through the windscreen and fallen between two rocks. That's apparently what saved my life.'*

What happened to the gold and the convoy might have remained a mystery for ever, had it not been for a small band of gypsies fleeing across the border to Hungary who had witnessed the whole attack, or the group of refugees who found Albert. Once they reached Budapest they told their story to the Polish Embassy. Tied in with what Albert said it was not difficult to piece together the fate of the gold or the men guarding it.

According to the gypsies the battle had lasted no more than half an hour. Lech and his men were hopelessly outnumbered and out-gunned. But not a man surrendered. Everyone from the convoy was killed.

The gypsies swore it was Russians who had attacked the convoy, although the refugees had brought in a dead SS officer. The gypsies, however, had seen the Russian uniforms, and watched horrified as they stripped one of the dead Poles and dressed him in the uniform of a German soldier, before a young Russian had repeatedly smashed the butt of his rifle down onto his head. They stayed long enough to see the Russians load all the other bodies onto trucks, and then, realising that they wouldn't survive if they were caught, hurried on their way down the pass to Hungary. It was a grim story, but few at the Embassy doubted it was true.

To this day the story has never been contradicted. Only the Russians know what happened to the gold, and their reasons for wanting the Poles to think that the Germans had taken it.

Commander Henry Payne stood on the bridge of the British destroyer and looked out over Trieste harbour. It was four o'clock on the afternoon of 26 September and for two reasons he was feeling restless. This was his first command and he had been bitterly disappointed when ordered to Trieste. The excitement of convoy patrol would have suited him much better. Secondly, it was beginning to look as if the Poles were not going to show up after all. 'Ah well,' he thought, 'at least the wait will soon be over.' For his orders were to leave Trieste in two days time and return to England with all speed.

He moved his stocky frame over to the map table and idly fingered a compass – the waiting had not suited him, and yet he desperately wanted the Poles to succeed. To see the trucks loaded with the gold coming along the dockside would be quite an experience. He would not often get the chance to carry such a valuable cargo on his ship!

'You're too impatient, Henry Payne,' he thought. 'and that could make a bad commander. You will have to watch yourself.'

'Sir.'

Startled, he swung round to see his signals officer by his side.

'God, man, don't sneak up on me like that!'

'Sorry, sir, but I thought you ought to see this immediately.'

Henry took the piece of paper and after a few seconds blew out his cheeks. 'Well I'll be damned!' he said out loud, causing all those on the bridge to turn and look at him.

'I'm sorry to tell you, gentlemen, that they haven't made it. Ambushed somewhere in the Carpathians. The message doesn't say by whom, but we can assume it was Germans. God, the poor bastards.'

He looked round at the sombre faces. Every man on the ship had been praying that the Poles would succeed.

Henry turned and looked back out across the harbour. He felt a twinge of sadness that he would not now be carrying the gold to America. He wondered what had happened to the Poles – probably he would never know. He shrugged his broad shoulders and turned back towards the men around him.

'Well, gentlemen, we can't stay here and allow the war to go on without us, can we? Prepare the ship to sail for England without delay.'

PART TWO

OCTOBER 1939 – APRIL 1945

Chapter 7

Albert owed his life to the group of refugees who, at great risk to themselves because he slowed their progress, unselfishly carried him down the mountains and into Hungary then on to Budapest, where they took him to the Polish Embassy. From there he was immediately transferred to hospital.

Weeks later when he had returned to Paris he wrote in his diary, *'I can remember nothing until I woke in a bed gazing at a cracked white ceiling. I was in pain and dazed: in fact, unable to remember anything. A pretty nurse, who spoke fluent Polish and looked after me like a little boy, told me I was in a Budapest hospital and had a lot of injuries. I just remember shouting at her every time she came into the room. All I wanted was my memory back. How she put up with me I will never know! I think I knew I had been through a terrible experience, but the cause eluded me, and led to the most appalling panics which hit me from time to time as I lay in this small white room. God, it was a funny feeling – I can remember it so clearly – and yet the past was blank! I seemed to think that I was about to be tortured – heaven knows why – apparently I had been brought in unconscious and when I regained consciousness I kept shouting that I was a prisoner of the Germans. Looking back on it now the hospital staff must have thought they had a lunatic in the bed. And so I think they might have had, but for the nurse's calming influence and the arrival of Jan Paderewski.'*

'Now, come on, Captain Mieszkowski, you have nothing to worry about. It is only someone from your Embassy.'

The nurse went over to the bed and took Albert's hand. 'It's all right, it's all right, I promise you.'

He closed his eyes and sighed – he was so tired, so confused. If only he could remember.

He whispered, 'How can he help me? Oh God, if only my bloody brain would work!'

She squeezed his hand. 'It will soon. It's just the shock. You were in a very bad way when you were brought in three days ago. You are a very lucky man to be alive, you know. If some of your countrymen hadn't found you when they did you would have soon been dead.'

He shook his head angrily. 'Where did they find me?'

'In the Tatras, on the road to a place called Mukacevo, I think they called it. You were unconscious, badly cut about the face and head and your left shoulder was dislocated. Added to that you were very cold and had lost a lot of blood.'

Something jogged his memory.

'Mukacevo?'

'Yes, I think so.'

He wrinkled his nose, trying to think. 'It's no good. For a moment there I thought I had something.' He beat his free arm on the white sheets in frustration. 'Tell me again how you knew my name.'

'Your passport was in the pocket of your uniform. Also a letter from a General Anders to you and Andre . . . oh, I can't remember his other name. The gentleman waiting to see you will be able to tell you.'

'I knew I was so close then,' wrote Albert, *'So bloody close – Andre, Mukacevo, the Tatras – there was a bell ringing in my brain. I had to know more.'*

'Let me call the man in,' said the nurse. 'Maybe he will be able to jog your brain.'

'Very well.'

The nurse smiled. 'I hoped you would say that. Now, first, let me get you sitting up in bed and looking presentable.'

She leaned over him and gently eased him off the pillows. *'The pain was excruciating, and the whole room seemed to spin in front of me,'* he wrote. *'I remember thinking, Oh God, I'm going to pass out.'*

But Albert recovered as the nurse hung on to him. 'Hold on,' she said crisply, 'The nausea will pass in a few moments.' She held him tightly until she felt him relax. 'Better?'

'Yes, I think so.' He moved his head gently from side to side. 'Yes, I'm okay now.'

She eased him back onto the pillows. 'Well done, you are certainly better today. That's the first time you haven't lost consciousness when I have attempted to sit you up. Now, try not to get too excited while I go and get the gentleman. If at any time you want him to leave, just say so. I will stay in the room.'

'*I remember saying something ridiculous like "you're an Angel, nurse". She patted my arm and said, "Not really – just doing my job."*

'*I was reluctant to see her go. My brain seemed to be working overtime and yet was coming up with nothing. And then there was the fear – how I remember that! I think it was the feeling that I was a prisoner. I know I nearly fainted, at least I think I did. If I had been able to write it down immediately then things might have been different. But it is nearly ten weeks later, and with all that has happened to me in the meantime I find my recollection of those days in hospital a little hazy.*'

The nurse took hold of Jan Paderewski's hand. 'Now, you must be careful with him, Mr Paderewski. He is still very weak. Treat him gently, and don't push a point if he seems confused. If after some minutes you are getting nowhere, I am under instructions from the doctors to ask you to leave. It means he will need a little more time.' The nurse gave him her most charming smile and led the way to Albert's room.

Jan Paderewski followed her apprehensively. It was not as if he was about to meet a stranger, for the man behind the door was one of his closest friends, but he had been warned of his state of mind and was all too well aware that he might be wasting his time. He was not looking forward to the next few minutes at all. Yet, if anybody could jog Albert's memory, it would certainly be him, and it was vital that he tried to get some sort of sense out of Albert if he could. For Jan had a lot of questions that desperately needed answering. He could only pray that they were not encased forever in Albert's brain.

As they reached the door and the nurse turned to him he unconsciously stepped back. Was he about to see a man who had been witness to so many horrors that his faculties had deliberately shut them away? Did he want to be the cause of that grief coming to the surface? Yet . . . he had a job to do. Something had gone very wrong somewhere and he had to know what it was. The letter proved that. Even though the Paris Embassy had refused to comment when contacted, and had become very secretive – it was understandable, he knew – there was so much suspicion everywhere. It had, however, been damnably frustrating. Even more so as his efforts to get through to Warsaw had met with no success. So it all depended on poor Albert. He took a deep breath, did his best to smile at the nurse, and followed her into the room.

In spite of steeling himself for something of a shock, he was quite unprepared for the ashen, shrunken face, with eyes so deeply set in their sockets that he could hardly see them. Or for the once wide, generous mouth sucked in, as if he had lost all his teeth and the large nose stitched from end to end. Or for the head shaven of hair, and criss-crossed with cuts going off at all angles on the scalp. He was not a pretty sight. To make matters worse, Jan was certain he could smell fear emanating from the skeleton-like figure lying in the bed.

'Albert,' he croaked as he moved forward.

Trembling under the bedclothes, Albert's eyes swept back and forth between the nurse and Jan. She touched Jan's arm and put a finger to her lips. She wanted to make Albert speak first. It didn't matter if it was a cry of joy or fear – she just wanted to be sure he was aware they were in the room.

Jan froze.

Albert gazed at him through his sunken eyes.

'Jan!' he managed to choke out, 'Jan, oh Jan! Christ Almighty, man, is it really you?'

The nurse smiled.

Jan felt a tear trickle down his cheek. 'You bet it is, old friend. And it's bloody good to see you alive!'

He hurried to the edge of the bed and put a hand on one of Albert's – it was as cold as steel. 'Tell me, what on earth you have been doing?'

Albert was speechless. Why was Jan Paderewski in Budapest? He thought he was in London. He shook his head to make sure he wasn't dreaming – no, he was still there and he had recognised him, that's what really mattered – by God, he was sane after all! London or Budapest, what did it matter. He was standing before him, flesh and blood. He looked up into the friendly eyes and tried to smile. 'I can't tell you how bloody wonderful it is to see you! But why are you here?'

'I had a change of posting the day after I saw you and Andre off at Lvov station. Do you remember? We drank too much schnapps and I nearly got on the train instead of you?'

Albert screwed up his eyes. 'So, you were going to London at one time?'

'Yes.'

Albert frowned. 'At least I got that bit right. So tell me about Andre – I just can't . . .' He stopped and looked pleadingly at Jan. 'I know I should remember.'

'Andre Zaluski. The three of us were inseparable. You must remember him, surely?'

Something clicked then; the brain cells, comatose for so long, suddenly woke up and threatened to overwhelm Albert with the horrors that had numbed his memory for so many days. He started to scream. He didn't want to stop, for the first vibrations were too horrible to countenance. He screamed again, and went on screaming until the needle pricked his arm, and the drug flowed through his veins, cutting off his brain from the rest of his nervous system.

Albert wrote in his diary, *'Even now I remember the awful feeling of despair and hopelessness. I think it will stay with me for the rest of my life. I can't remember screaming – Jan told me that the next day – but I can remember seeing Andre's face covered in blood beside me.'*

The next day Jan returned to the hospital in the early afternoon, and was met by the same nurse who had hurriedly escorted him out of Albert's room the day before.

'I think I'm expected, nurse. A doctor rang the Embassy to say that I could visit Albert today.'

'Yes, yes. I'm delighted to say he is much better. He seems to have come to terms with himself and we think he remembers everything. He is reluctant to talk to any of us. I think it will be different with a friend. One word of caution though. He may get a little excited. He is very worked up and we don't want him to have a relapse.'

Jan nodded, and they walked together as far as Albert's door. 'I will leave you now,' she said. 'Good luck, Mr Paderewski.'

Before he could say a word she was gone. He could feel his heart hammering against his ribs – it was too stupid! He had to be in perfect control. The last thing he wanted to do was telegraph his anxiety to Albert. He took a deep breath and pushed open the door.

Albert was sitting up in bed looking a very different man to the day before. His eyes were clearer and he managed a smile. Jan felt some of the tension leave him.

Albert half raised a hand. 'My God, Jan, am I glad to see you again. Sorry about yesterday – I think I made a bloody fool of myself.' He swallowed hard and looked down at the sheets. There was still a deep nagging pain in his stomach. 'My God, it still hurts to think of what happened to Andre. In some ways I wish I had never remembered.' He forced himself to look at Jan. 'Well, you didn't come here to listen to me moaning, did you! Where do you want me to start?'

Jan pulled the only chair in the room over to the bed. 'I expect you will find this hard to believe, but we know very little here. You were brought across the border by a group of refugees, who found you and a dead German soldier. We found a letter on you sent to you and Andre in Paris written by General Anders. I couldn't get through to Warsaw, so I tried the Ambassador in Paris. Nothing, you would have thought, could have been simpler. But as soon as we mentioned you and Andre and Warsaw he shut up like a clam – said he could trust no one unless he met them face to face, and why if you were here couldn't we get all the information from you. I tried to explain but he wouldn't listen. I seemed to throw him into a complete panic. So we were "up a gum tree" as you might say, until two days ago, when some gypsies stopped off at the Embassy with a very strange story about a Russian ambush on a convoy of lorries. They said everyone in the convoy was killed and loaded onto the trucks, except for one body that was stripped and put into the uniform of a German lieutenant. To tell you the truth, it all seems a bit far fetched. But then, why bother to make it up and come specially to tell us at the Embassy? Anyway, I have a feeling you know most of the answers. Is that not right?'

Albert reached out and gripped Jan's hand. 'You know nothing more?'

'Nothing.'

'My God, Jan, tell me the date.'

'September 26th.'

Albert's nails dug into Jan's wrist and when he spoke his voice sounded very excited. 'The destroyer, Jan, the bloody destroyer!'

Jan pulled his hand away and rubbed his wrist. 'Calm down, Albert, please. It's no good talking to me in riddles. Why not start from the moment you and Andre left Paris.'

For a moment he feared that Albert was on the verge of hysteria and he had half risen from his chair to go to call the nurse when Albert said urgently, 'Wait! I'll be okay in a second. I just need a drink.' He reached out to the bedside table and took the half full glass of water with a shaking hand. He drank slowly, giving himself time to calm down.

'Right,' he said with a weak smile, 'I'm ready now.'

Jan felt impatience building up inside him. But he knew it would be fatal to hurry his friend. 'In your own time, Albert – I have the rest of the day.'

As the story unfolded, Jan had difficulty in not interrupting several times, but he sensed that if he stopped the flow, Albert might never be able to continue. So he sat mesmerised for half an hour without uttering a word.

'The last thing I remember . . .' Albert choked. 'Oh Christ . . . is Andre's mutilated head landing on my lap. Oh God, Jan!'

Jan was lost for words. He simply shook his head and took hold of Albert's hand.

'We should have been in Trieste by the 20th!' continued Albert. 'I wonder if Lech made it. If the gypsies' story is to be believed, he is dead as well. So the poor bloody English are probably still waiting for us! You must get on to them and find out what has happened.'

'If they are still there,' said Jan, a trifle breathlessly.

'Oh, they will be if Lech hasn't arrived,' Albert assured him. 'They had orders to wait until the 28th.'

Jan leant over the bed. 'Look, Albert, this is all news to me. Of course we can get nothing out of the German Embassy here. All I can say is that they have told the Hungarians that they have no troops in that part of Poland.'

'If only I could remember more!' cried Albert. 'But it's no good; Andre slumping dead on my lap is my last memory. After that . . . God only knows.'

'I understand. But if the convoy hasn't reached Trieste, we must assume that the gypsies' story is true, and that everyone with it has been killed and the gold hijacked by the Russians.'

'That does seem the most likely answer, I admit,' said Albert, looking puzzled. 'If it was Germans, why would they leave one of their men behind? What about me? How did I evade them?'

'Well, at least I can answer that. You had fallen between two large rocks. If one of your rescuers hadn't gone to relieve himself you would never have been found. You were bloody lucky.'

'Not really. I have failed, Jan, and probably lost two good friends. I should have been killed with them.'

Albert fell silent and Jan got up from his chair. 'That is utter nonsense, and the sooner you stop thinking like that the better. Now, listen, I hate to leave you like this, but I'm sure you understand your story is of some importance and I must get back to the Embassy. First I will check out Trieste. And please, Albert, don't blame yourself – you did your best – no one could have asked for more.'

'You may be right. But the thought of those bloody bastards having the gold! . . . Ah! I remember something now! Yes, of course! It was the Russians we feared might catch up with us, not the Germans. The Russians, Jan! It must have been the Russians. I bet they wanted to put the blame on the Germans – hence the lieutenant. It makes sense.'

Jan rubbed his chin. 'I think you're right. In that case the gypsies were telling the truth. I will make some enquiries. I have a few reliable contacts and I would just like to make sure there were no German troops in the Tatras at the time.'

Albert shrugged. 'Well, it doesn't matter much anyway. If the gold has gone, it's gone. It's almost immaterial who took it.' He was growing tired.

Realising this, Jan hurried on. 'Now listen, try not to worry about Andre or Lech or the Russians. I will check out everything and come and see you again tomorrow. Get some rest and then the sooner you will get out of here.'

'What will I do then?' Albert asked despondently.

'Plenty of time to think of that when you are better. You are welcome at the Embassy and that is where you should make any decisions, not here. Now, I really must go. Shall I call that pretty nurse?'

'Please. I don't feel like being alone. And Jan?'

'Yes?'

'No sign of my family, I presume?'

'No. Were they heading here?'

'I don't know. I just thought . . .' His voice trailed off.

'I'll see what I can find out. Now, for God's sake stop worrying. You must rest or your wounds will never heal.'

Albert gave him a weak smile. 'To tell you the truth, I don't care very much at the moment.'

'You will,' said Jan as he made for the door. Outside in the passage he ran into the nurse, who was about to go off duty. She smiled when she saw him. 'How is the patient?'

'He told me an intriguing story. But I have left him rather tired and depressed. He wants to see you, but I can see you are just leaving.'

She touched his arm. 'Don't worry, I don't mind staying. I hadn't got anything special planned.'

'You're an angel.'

She laughed. 'Do all you Poles say that?'

Jan gave her a questioning look.

'That's what your friend called me,' she replied.

Jan laughed. 'I think he was right. Perhaps it would help if I knew your name?'

'Anna.'

'The Angel Anna,' he teased. 'It sounds nice. Perhaps one day you will allow me to say "thank you" by taking you out to dinner?'

'That would be very nice, Mr Paderewski.'

'Jan, please.'

She laughed and, turning away, called over her shoulder. 'Very well, Jan, see you tomorrow, no doubt.'

'Absolutely no doubt.'

'*When Jan left,*' wrote Albert, '*I felt so dreadful that if I'd had the means at my finger tips I think I would have killed myself. I kept thinking of Andre and Lech and of how disappointed General Anders would be with us. I was not thinking rationally then, I know, but even now I haven't quite shaken off the feeling of loss and failure.*'

It wasn't until late the next afternoon that Jan was able to get back to the hospital and by that time Albert was finding it difficult to contain his impatience.

'*I was in a foul mood,*' he wrote, '*I started swearing at Jan for taking so long in getting back. When I saw him throw a look at Anna, who was standing by the window, I lost control of myself. I remember shouting at them for ignoring me, and that it was all right for them because they didn't have to lie in bed thinking about their dead friends. I knew I was being irrational but couldn't have cared less. I just wanted somebody to hit out at and work off my feeling of utter despair. I wouldn't have blamed them if they had walked out. But Anna just smiled and walked up to my bed and shook her head. Between them they calmed me down and Jan then told me why he was later than he had expected. Warsaw had surrendered at 2.00 p.m. It was the end for Poland, and for all those caught in the city, especially the Jews. I was devastated – worried about my family – and overwhelmed by a feeling of loss. My beloved country was in the hands of barbarians. And the bad news didn't stop there. No one had arrived at Trieste and so the British destroyer had sailed empty-handed. The gypsies' story was confirmed. Somewhere deep inside Russia was the gold and the bodies of my two friends. I remember crying then, and they left me curled up in the bed, alone with my misery.*

'*As I write this I still can't shake off the ghosts of Andre and Lech, and I'm wondering if they will ever get a decent burial. Oh God, this bloody war! When will it end?*'

Chapter 8

It was another two weeks before Albert was discharged from hospital. He'd had the greatest difficulty in controlling his restlessness, but Jan had visited him every day to give him a run-down on any new developments. During the first week General Wladyslaw Sikorski had set up a Polish government in exile in Paris, and reports were coming through that the German army had not yet entered Warsaw.

'The rumour is they are terrified of what they might find,' said Jan. 'I shudder to think what we may hear next.'

'So, no luck in getting through to General Anders to report the loss of the gold?' asked Albert.

'None.'

The second week brought a rash of desperate news from Warsaw which did nothing to help Albert's frame of mind.

'The Germans have gone into Warsaw,' reported a disconsolate Jan. 'And from the little information that we are getting, the plight of the people is terrible. A conservative estimate coming out of Poland is that at least 15,000 civilians have been killed in Warsaw alone. What must the carnage be throughout the whole country? Added to that, we heard last night that the Germans are already claiming they have nearly eradicated the Polish upper class and the clergy – it seems to be mass murder on a terrifying scale.'

Albert held his head in his hands. 'No news, I suppose, of my family?'

'Not yet, I'm afraid.'

'I fear time could be running out on them,' said Albert. 'Dear God, Jan! Where on earth are our Allies! Can't anyone help us?'

'It's far too late. Although a communiqué has come through from our Embassy in London saying that the British and French governments have expressed their deep shock to our respective Ambassadors at the fate of our country. They are particularly angry at the connivance of the Soviets in the partition of a State which only a short while ago was independent. Also, our Ambassador has been told that there is a certain amount of shame in both capitals that they did not help us more.'

'Ha!' exclaimed Albert bitterly. 'A fat lot of good that does us now!'

Jan nodded in agreement.

Albert walked out of what had increasingly seemed to him like prison on the morning of 10 October. He shook hands with the two doctors who had been instrumental in returning him to something like good health before turning to Anna, who was standing a little to one side watching him with a wistful eye. In the time that she had nursed him, she had discovered, beneath the wounded exterior of a man being torn to pieces by the loss of good friends and the worry about his family, a warm and gentle character who, in spite of her normally controlled defence, had eaten deep under her skin until he had touched her heart. She would miss him – the first time she could say that of any of the patients she had nursed.

'And you, Anna, how can I thank you?'

She smiled and looked at the floor.

'If it hadn't been for you, I know I would never have recovered.'

'Oh, what rubbish, of course you would. I only did what any nurse would do.'

Albert shook his head. 'Maybe, but it was how you did it.' He moved quickly, and before she knew it she was in his arms and he was planting a kiss firmly on her lips. For a split second she relaxed and then over Albert's shoulder she caught the eye of one of the doctors.

She pushed him away. 'Please . . .'

Realising that he had embarrassed her he was quick to apologise. 'I'm sorry – but that is how I feel. I owe you a lot and I will never forget you. Goodbye, Anna, and thank you.'

He turned away and nodded to Jan, who was standing by the Embassy car. 'Let's go, then.'

Once seated in the car he looked round to wave and felt a slight pang of regret when he saw Anna was gone. 'Quite a girl, that,' he said to Jan as the car pulled away.

His friend just nodded as he joined the flow of traffic.

The first things that struck Albert were the streets packed with people and the shops bulging with food and other goods.

'War hasn't hit them yet?' he asked Jan.

'Not yet. You will be surprised by the atmosphere here. The Hungarians are determined to enjoy themselves for as long as they can. But underneath this rather brash surface is a deep feeling of unease. Nevertheless, I have learnt that no Hungarian will give up the chance to sing and dance until death is staring him or her in the face. They have a wonderfully carefree attitude towards life – don't be fooled by their seemingly austere exterior, for inside every Hungarian is a bit of gypsy blood pumping away to get out and burst into song. I have decided they are a very happy people.'

'Can they stay out of the war?'

Jan shook his head. 'Who knows? Frankly, given their geographical position, I doubt it. However their Prime Minister, Pal Teleki, is determined to try.'

'If they come in, it will be on the side of the Germans?'

'Without a doubt. We have to appreciate, they have little choice, and already Germany's influence is quite obvious. Such as the fact that you will have to report to the police fairly soon. They like to keep a check on any Poles that come into the country. There is nothing to worry about at the moment, as you have your passport, but we are constantly on our guard for changes.'

Twenty minutes later they arrived at the Embassy, and as Albert got shakily out of the car and looked up at the building his eyes swam with tears. He was still weak and constantly thought of Andre and Lech, and as he gratefully accepted the guiding hand of Jan and allowed himself to be led like a blind man towards the entrance, he knew he had to put the last few weeks to the back of his mind as quickly as possible before he allowed himself to drift into a state of constant self-pity. It wouldn't be easy, but somehow he had to draw on all his reserves of willpower to make it possible.

In the 1930s Budapest had expanded like a balloon. The rural population had shrunk dramatically and the city had continued to grow. By 1939 more than a million Hungarians, nearly an eighth of the country's population, were jammed into the city.

Overcrowded as it was, Budapest was still beautiful, with the Danube cutting through the heart of the city, distancing the historic Buda Hills from the elegant boulevards of Pest, yet linking and enhancing the beauty of the whole. Its dramatic setting made Budapest one of Europe's most romantic cities.

To Albert, struggling to put some meaning back into his life, it provided the ideal atmosphere to lift the gloom off his young shoulders and, skilfully handled by Jan, he slowly felt himself becoming a human being again.

By the end of his first week out of hospital, Albert had reported to the police and been put under no restrictions. And in spite of the horror stories filtering out of Poland of more German atrocities, and although there was still no news of his family, he found he was beginning to unwind by strolling the wide boulevards and sitting in one of the many coffee houses that Jan took him to each day in the early afternoon. It was good therapy to sip coffee and eat strudel while listening to someone playing a violin and watching the people fighting for space on the overcrowded pavements.

He soon learnt that Hungarians conformed to no stereotype in their physical appearance. There were high-cheekboned blondes and round-faced brunettes. There were swarthy men with droopy moustaches and blue-eyed red-heads just to confuse the issue. He noticed with a wry smile that the middle-aged were beginning to show the toll of all the strudel snacks, which seemed to be on constant offer wherever he and Jan went.

In fact, he thought, Budapest was a bit like Paris. Not only because of its shops, restaurants and beautiful buildings, but because she, too, seemed determined to head helter-skelter towards inevitable destruction with gay abandon.

On 19 October, the Embassy heard that all Poles had been expelled from the port and city of Gdynia, twenty kilometres from Gdansk, and from towns throughout the area annexed by the Germans, with only as many possessions as they could carry, and ordered to find new homes in parts of Poland that were already starving. Jan suggested that they should go to the State Opera that evening to try and cheer themselves up. He had got to know the Prima Donna, Helene Milosevo, through a Hungarian friend of his who was connected with the Opera in Budapest. 'She has a lovely voice,' he assured Albert, 'and easy on the eye as well.'

That night as they crossed the Danube from Central Budapest by the Elizabeth Bridge, the true beauty of the city struck Albert, and he was feeling as relaxed as ever he had done since leaving hospital as Jan braked to a halt outside the Opera house. Albert stretched before getting out of the car and realised that he was really looking forward to the evening.

The Állami Operaház, an imposing piece of architecture, sits proudly at the river end of the Ándrassy Útja, a magnificent tree-lined avenue nearly 2.5 kilometres long. Built in the late 1870s, it was designed on the lines of the Champs-Elysées in Paris. Albert would have liked to have spent longer looking down its length, but he was hurried into the foyer of the Opera House by Jan and led towards an impressive staircase winding up to the boxes and assembly rooms. Halfway up Jan turned him to look at sixteen statues of great opera composers high above the entrance. 'The one second to the right is of Franz Liszt,' said Jan. 'Next to him is Ferenc Erkel, whom you may not have heard about, but he composed the Hungarian National Anthem and was director of the Opera House when it opened in 1884. Everyone in Budapest is proud of these two men.'

Once they had taken their seats Albert had time to look around at the interior. Although it was luxurious, it was not in bad taste, and the splendid four-tiered gallery added to its magnificence. He sat back with a sigh and opened his programme.

They had come to listen to Puccini's *Turandot*. Always amongst his favourites, Albert was looking forward to hearing Helene Milosovo sing the part of the Chinese princess, Turandot. He wondered if she was as good as Jan had claimed. From her photograph she was certainly most attractive, and he was much looking forward to meeting her after the performance, as Jan had promised he would.

From the moment she came on the stage she captivated him. Every note she sang seemed to go to his heart and he simply could not take his eyes off her. The sheer joy with which she sang overwhelmed him and his eyes had already misted over as the chorus sang the rousing finale. It had always stirred his blood like no other piece of music and he knew the words by heart.

> Amor!
> O sole! Vita! Eternità!
> Luce del mondo e amore!
> Ride e canto nel sole
> l'infinità nostra felicità!
> Gloria a te! Gloria a te! Gloria!

The music and the singing rang true and clear around the great auditorium and Albert was not the only one unashamedly crying into his handkerchief as the last notes died away.

'My God, that was marvellous!' he shouted to Jan as Helene Milosovo took her first curtain call. 'What a voice – what a woman!'

He clapped until the palms of his hands were sore, and as he watched her disappear behind the curtain for the last time, he was already on the way to being in love with her.

In her dressing-room, he held back, not sure of how he would react when introduced, but she had spotted him the moment he had come into the room, and been struck by his good looks and the rather arrogant way he surveyed the room. Once the handful of fawning admirers had dropped away she wasted no time in going over to where he was talking to Jan.

'Jan,' she said in a rather husky voice, 'How lovely to see you here tonight. Did you enjoy yourself?'

'As ever, when I hear you sing,' he replied.

'Oh, you flatterer! And who is your friend?'

'Helene, may I introduce Albert Mieszkowski, a great friend of mine who has just come out of Poland.'

'Oh, you poor man,' she said, touching his arm, 'Did you have a terrible time?'

'If you don't mind, I would rather not talk about it right now, especially when I have just sat enraptured by your singing,' said Albert. 'I have always loved *Turandot*, but never as much as I did tonight.' He gave a little bow and smiled uneasily. His heart was beating too fast.

'You are too kind, but it is nice to have a new, and so handsome, an admirer. Would you care to have dinner with me tonight?'

Taken aback by her direct approach, Albert just stared at her.

'Well?'

'Yes, yes, of course I would love to.'

'Wonderful. You don't mind, Jan, do you? I will see that your friend is delivered home by dawn.'

Albert swallowed. He hadn't thought he would be on his own. He shot a look of panic at Jan, who merely smiled and slapped him on the back.

'Of course not, Helene.' He winked at Albert. 'It will do him the world of good.'

Albert, desperately trying to control his panic-ridden excitement, took the opportunity to look in more detail at the woman opposite him as she turned away to talk to another man who had come up beside her. He guessed she might be around thirty, but her age, he reflected, did not matter; what did, was her beauty. With her long, dark hair cascading down over her finely-made face, now washed clean of any makeup, onto her bare shoulders, she stood inches taller than anyone else in the room except himself. Her figure was full, with large bosoms straining tantalisingly from behind her bodice. Her eyes flashed erotically and her voice, like her singing, was soft and lyrical. He decided she had a definite look of the gypsy about her, and that he had never set eyes on such a magnificent woman.

So there started an affair of such intensity that both of them almost forgot there was a war raging around them. From the start, neither of them had any illusions that one day it would end. For different reasons both were intent on wiping away past unhappiness, although Albert was never sure what it was with her, but every now and then, in their more intimate moments, she nearly told him. He never forced her confidence, for he had a feeling if he had done, she would walk away just as quickly as she had taken him to her bed.

'It isn't going to last,' he said to an incredulous Jan, only a week after their first meeting. 'We both know this, so why wait? Enjoy ourselves in the short time we have together, for tomorrow either one of us could be dead.'

Jan shook his head and said nothing. He was glad that someone had come along to lift Albert's gloom; he hadn't expected it to happen so suddenly, or to be Helene Milosevo. But he reckoned it didn't matter who it was – Albert's philosophy made sense. Besides, it gave him more time to turn his attentions to Anna, who he'd been seeing quite regularly since Albert left the hospital.

From that first night of *Turandot*, Albert never missed an evening when Helene was singing, and afterwards, once she had shaken off the usual gaggle of admirers, it was off to one restaurant or another, and then, as they had done even on their first night, it was back across the river to her bed in an old house in the Castle district. It was there that Albert discovered her body was as soft as her singing.

'If the world had been at peace,' he wrote in his diary, *'We might have moved slower. Our love-making perhaps not quite so urgent. Our desire to find out all we could about each other, and to discuss our joy of music, not quite so intense. But the shadows grew larger and blacker every day so we had no time for the niceties of a gentle courtship.'*

The days flew by for Albert – the worry for his family not quite so painful, and the memories of Andre and Lech shifted more onto their characters rather than on their untimely deaths. At times he told himself that it was wrong to be happy, but it was impossible to be anything else in Helene's presence, and whenever he mentioned his guilt, she would put a finger to his lips and shake her head.

How long the affair would have lasted was something that Albert many years on could never answer. The only person he ever confided in was his son John, but otherwise he kept Helene locked up in his heart, like some treasure that he was frightened to expose to the outside world.

In fact, it lasted a month, and came to an end not because they were tired of each other, but because the Hungarian authorities, under increasing pressure from the Germans, decided to intern all Poles living in their country.

Thanks to Jan, Albert got early warning of their intentions, and decided to get out of the country before he was picked up. There had been too many stories of Poles going missing for him to be prepared to risk internment without first trying to get away.

He knew there was no hope of Helene coming with him, and their last night together was indicative of the approach that the couple had taken to their liaison from the beginning. Their sadness was hidden in their joy of having known each other, and of the knowledge that they had been lucky enough to find such fleeting happiness. Their farewell the next morning was not tearful, nor particularly emotional. Albert told Jan it was like a parting of two friends, convinced they would meet again at some other time and place.

Jan, who had been expecting to be faced with an almost suicidal friend, was once again lost for words.

Chapter 9

Albert's plan was to cross the border into Yugoslavia and make for Trieste via Zagreb where he hoped to find a boat to take him to Marseille and from there back to the Embassy in Paris. He felt that, if his family was still alive, their only chance now stood in getting to France, and if this happened he wanted to be there.

Jan drove him as far as the border town of Letenye, as close to Zagreb as he could get without actually crossing into Yugoslavia – something he was reluctant to risk as it was imperative that he returned to the Embassy safely. The rest was up to Albert, who had decided to take a gamble on the Hungarian guards turning a blind eye to one Pole with a passport. This assumption was based on two reasons: firstly, the speed with which Jan had alerted him, and secondly, the reported reluctance of the Hungarian authorities to carry out the Nazi edict. Given the remoteness of the border post, he felt it was far less of a risk than trying to sneak across at night and ending up either shot or a prisoner.

Once again he found himself saying goodbye to a close friend. 'I worry about leaving you,' he said to Jan as he got out of the car, 'I would hate to think that you might be interned.'

'That should be the least of your worries right now,' replied Jan. 'Just make sure you get across into Yugoslavia first. I'm sure everyone at the Embassy will be all right, and besides, we must remain at least until we are sure we cannot be of any further use to the Poles here.'

Albert was filled with doubt, but kept his mouth shut. He knew whatever he said Jan would ignore. He felt a bit like a traitor as they embraced. 'I cannot possibly thank you enough for all your kindness, I hope we will meet again one day.'

'I, too – and good luck, old friend. I hope you make it. And don't worry, I will try and keep you informed about Helene.'

As he had hoped, Albert encountered no difficulty getting across the border, and six weeks later, on 28 December, he arrived in France. On the second day of 1940, he reached Paris and made for the Embassy. It had taken him longer than he had planned because he had been held up in Trieste, but at least he was still a free man.

He was greeted with surprise and elation at the Embassy, and no one was happier to see him than Josef Milosz. Like everyone else, they thought he had failed to get out of Hungary.

'Sit down, sit down, boy,' said Josef, pointing at the familiar chair. 'I never thought I would see you again.'

Albert gave him a tired smile. 'Nor I you, sir, at times,' he said, collapsing into the chair. Suddenly he felt very lonely. The room was full of too many memories.

'Any news of . . .'

Josef finished the sentence for him. 'Your family. Yes, indeed.'

Albert sat bolt upright, his tiredness forgotten. 'You mean they are safe!'

'I do. And by now they should be in England. They came here three weeks ago. Of course, we could not get in touch with you. In fact, I fear they think you are either dead or a prisoner somewhere. It was the natural assumption. I tried to persuade them that it would take you a long time to get here but, to be honest, I think they almost wanted to assume the worst. Do you know what I mean?'

Albert was openly crying and could only manage to choke out, 'Yes, yes, I think so.' He pulled out a handkerchief and wiped his eyes. 'Sorry . . . but you have no idea how I feel.'

Josef smiled. 'Oh, I think I do, young man, I think I do.'

'I must contact them immediately.'

'Of course. I have already put a call through to our Embassy in London and they will ring back within the hour.'

Albert shuffled his feet. 'God, sir, an hour?'

'An hour because they have to find them. They stayed at the Embassy for a few days but have now moved to a house in London.'

'I see. How were they when you saw them?'

'Well. A little tired, naturally. I gather your sister had just married and her husband helped them escape. But you will want to hear all of this from them direct.'

Albert laughed. 'She married him, then! Well, well!' He looked around the room, his eyes still swimming with tears. He felt as if a great weight had been lifted off his shoulders. Oh, if only Andre . . .

'Do you want to know what happened to Andre?'

The change of subject surprised Josef. 'Andre? Yes, yes, you had better tell me.'

Albert sat back in the chair and clasped his hands together. 'I expect you know quite a lot already from our Embassy in Budapest?'

Josef nodded. 'At first I was very suspicious. Gave nothing away until I was sure they were genuine – I had to be very careful, you understand. The value of the gold, and the chaos that was going on in Poland.'

Albert remembered Jan complaining. 'Of course.' He stopped to blow his nose. 'Andre is dead, and so, I fear, are all the brave men who came out of Warsaw with us and the gold. We were ambushed by Russians. A band of gypsies fleeing across the border saw the whole thing. The gold is lost.'

'I gathered that. The Russians! Who would have believed that. But you tried, Albert – that was all we expected of you. As for Andre – he will be a great loss.'

'He was a good friend. I shall miss him.'

'I'm sure. Now let me bring you up to date on events. I expect you are a little behind.'

A fleeting smile passed across Albert's face. 'Yes. I haven't had much time just recently to read the papers.'

'There is very little good news,' Josef began. 'Poland is being slowly strangled by the Nazis. We hear of more and more atrocities, especially to the Jews, and this can only be the tip of the iceberg. It is very difficult to get any reliable information out of the country, but of the confirmed reports is one that all males between 14 and 60 have been forced to work on what the Germans call "Labour Projects". You can imagine what that means. Another says that the Jews in Warsaw are having a terrible time. Do you know, Albert, I think Hitler wants to wipe all Jews off the face of the earth.'

He stopped briefly and started rummaging around in the mass of papers on his desk. 'I have a copy of a German article in one of their magazines somewhere here. Ah, got it. Let me read it to you.' He adjusted his glasses. '"Behind all the enemies of Germany's ascendancy, stand those who demand our encirclement – the oldest enemies of the German people and of all healthy, rising nations – the Jews".' Josef looked up at Albert. 'Have you ever heard anything so sinister?'

'Frightening.'

'Indeed, young man, and God help the world if that man isn't stopped soon.'

'Has anything more developed on the war front?' asked Albert.

'Hitler is still rattling his sabre. Making more noise than ever now that he escaped a bomb in Munich.'

'Someone tried to assassinate him?'

'Apparently. Needless to say, reports are very vague. It seems he went back to Munich to celebrate his "Putsch" of 1923, and someone had planted a bomb near the dais from which he was going to speak. Of course it must have gone wrong, as he is still alive, and rumour has it that the culprit has been caught.'

'Poor bugger,' said Albert with feeling.

'My sentiments exactly,' said Josef. 'However, I have one piece of good news to end on. Last month the German pocket battle ship *Graf Spee* was sunk by the British Navy. Something at least for us all to celebrate. Now how about . . .'

There was a knock on the door and Josef's secretary came in. 'Your father is on the line, Mr Mieszkowski!'

His father's voice was breaking with emotion and Albert knew he was having trouble speaking. 'Albert – dear God! We had given you up for dead.'

Albert heard him choke and the line went silent. A second later he heard Barbara's voice. 'I'm sorry, Albert, but both mother and father are too emotional to speak to you. It's as if you have come back from the dead.' Then even his normally calm sister broke down, 'Oh God, I can't tell you how wonderful it is to hear your voice,' she sobbed. 'Are you really okay?'

'I'm fine, just fine, darling sister. Except that I had given you all up for dead as well. Was it bad? Did you have trouble? How did you get away?'

'Hey, hey, one question at a time please!'

'Sorry, but . . .'

Her voice was controlled now. He could imagine her making an enormous effort – she had never liked to show him her weaknesses. 'I know. The answer is it was not bad at all. Thanks to Kasimir. We came out with remnants of the army. He is with us now and about to go to Scotland with some of the army units. I think father is tempted to follow. Oh, and by the way, I'm pregnant.'

'Good God!' exclaimed Albert. 'And I haven't even had a chance to congratulate you on your marriage! So a double celebration, eh? When's the baby due?'

'Not until May, which is a good thing, as it will give us a chance to find a home and get settled down. Everyone is being so helpful here.'

'Good. Are you short of money?'

'Not really. Of course it is not like being at Mieszki Wielkie. But friends have lent us enough to get by on until father can sell some of the jewellery we brought out of Poland. Don't worry, we will be fine.'

'Well, I hope everything works out for you and Kasimir.'

'It will. It has to. However, enough of that. We got to the Embassy all in one piece. Mother was very tired and father moaning that he hadn't brought his pipes or tobacco! It was a bit of a blow not to find any of our furniture or valuables – you were right there. So, thank goodness father hadn't sent the jewellery. Then we heard you were safe in Budapest. We were just celebrating that when we heard that all Poles in Hungary would be interned. That was a terrible blow to us. We were certain you would be picked up and eventually die. We felt so damned helpless, and as father felt we were in the way at the Embassy and couldn't help you, we decided to leave for England.'

'But the Embassy in Budapest knew that I was trying to get back to France and a friend drove me to the border.'

'They never told us a thing. I expect they had to be very careful what they said.'

'I suppose so.' Albert felt a cold hand touch his heart. Jan would almost certainly have told them. With an effort he continued. 'How cruel for you. I'm so sorry, Barbara.'

'It wasn't your fault. Besides, what does it matter now. You are alive! Are you coming over to England?'

Albert hesitated. He hadn't had time to think of what he might do. Stay at the Embassy, join the Polish army in exile? He felt he didn't want to commit himself.

'I'm not sure. You see, I've lost a lot of friends to the Germans. I have a feeling I should stay and fight.'

'You can fight them from England. Already there are many young Poles here.'

Albert felt a little trapped. 'Give me time, will you, Barbara? Please try to understand.'

'I will. But . . . think of father and mother before making any hasty decisions. Please, Albert.'

'Of course I will. Now, one other thing before I go. As you know, I began keeping a diary in 1938. I've kept it meticulously ever since, although I have a bit of catching up to do at the moment, as I left it here when I went to Warsaw. Thank God I did. Once I have brought it up to date, could I send it to you? I don't want to lose it, which I might if I try to keep it with me. It will be safer in your hands.'

'Of course. I hope, however, this doesn't mean you have already decided what to do. As we are not sure where we will be living I suggest you send it to the Embassy and then they can send it on to me.'

'Okay. I will feel happier with it out of the way. And don't worry, I haven't yet made up my mind. Now I think we had better stop. This telephone is very busy these days. Give my love to father and mother – I will speak to them when they have had time to calm down. Look after them, Barbara.'

He could tell she was near to tears again. 'I will, I promise. Goodbye, Albert. Don't stay away from us for too long.'

'I'll try not to. Goodbye, sister, take care of yourselves.'

The line went dead and he replaced the receiver thoughtfully.

'How were they?' asked Josef.

'Fine, fine.' He was thinking of Jan. 'I can't understand our Embassy in Budapest. They knew I was trying to get across the border and a friend had taken me there. I wonder why he didn't say anything. Can I ring them?'

'I'm sorry,' replied Josef. 'They stopped taking calls a week ago, and I have since heard that our Embassy has been closed. No news of the Ambassador or any of his staff yet.'

Albert shook his head. Had he lost yet another friend? He knew that Jan must be in trouble. All he could do was hope he survived.

That night in the quietness of his bedroom he brought his diary up to date, and then, tired as he was, he wrote to Helene. 'Why is it that I lose so many friends and get parted from the ones I love? I feel lonely and afraid. I know we agreed to have no regrets about our parting, but at this moment, I wish to God you were beside me. I hate that bastard in Berlin for parting us and for causing the deaths of people close to me. As you know, I'm not a violent man, but I wish I could kill him with my bare hands.'

Many years later he confided to his son John that he doubted if the affair with Helene would ever have come to anything. 'But,' he said, turning to him with a smile, 'She gave me the strength to go on when I felt the world was against me, and there is still a little bit of her here.' He thumped his heart with a fist.

In fact he carried in his wallet until the day he died, the crumpled photograph that he had torn out of the programme on his first visit to the Opera House to hear her sing *Turandot*.

Chapter 10

By February 1940 the West was fully aware of the German terror in the East. Details of most atrocities were now smuggled through within days, for neutral diplomats in Berlin were well informed, and public wall posters in Poland openly publicised executions. Mass executions had become Hitler's tool to subdue the Polish population.

When the Embassy in Paris heard that four thousand incurable patients from Polish mental hospitals had been eliminated, and that reliable information from eye witnesses put the death toll of Polish civilians at about fifteen thousand since the outbreak of war, a feeling of shock and revulsion swept over everyone. This savagery cut deep into Albert's heart, and it was the reason why, after much soul searching, he decided not to make for England, but to stay on French soil and join the 200,000 men of the Polish army who had escaped to France mainly through Roumania.

To his surprise his parents took the news calmly. *'I was amazed,'* he wrote in his diary after the war, *'that they were both so reasonable. I had certainly expected mother to become hysterical. It made me feel much more at ease with myself, and softened the blow of knowing that I would miss the birth of Barbara's baby.'*

In the early hours of 9 April 1940 German forces set foot on Norwegian and Danish soil. In Paris, Albert, who had been growing impatient for action, was forced to twiddle his thumbs for a few weeks longer before the German onslaught on France began. It was in stark contrast to the bitter fighting raging in Norway. He found this 'phoney peace' difficult to stomach, especially as the killing of Jews and Poles continued unabated. His restlessness was shared by his fellow countrymen, who could not wait to face their hated enemy once again. When, on 10 May, German forces advanced into Belgium and Holland, Albert felt that at last their chance would not be long in coming.

That afternoon he rang his father for what proved to be the last time until after the war. 'The balloon has well and truly gone up now, father,' he said, 'At last, we may get a chance to fight.'

'Take care,' came back the inadequate reply. 'And, by the way, we hope to move to Scotland in a week. Oh yes, Barbara says your diary has arrived.'

'Good. And be sure to try and get a message to the Embassy when the baby arrives. With luck they might be able to contact me. Give my love to mother, and tell Barbara that I will be praying for her. Au revoir, father.'

'As I put the telephone down I was overcome by a feeling of utter desolation,' he wrote. *'Was I ever to see my family again? It is easy now, with the war over, and reunited with them, to think that I was over-reacting. At the time, I was convinced I would be killed within the next few months.'*

The men of the 1st Polish Division to which Albert had been assigned were forced to kick their heels outside Paris for a little longer and the fact that they were assured that their chance would soon come did nothing to allay their frustration.

By 15 May the French had begun to panic as the German juggernaut rolled ruthlessly on, and the French Prime Minister, Paul Reynaud, rang Churchill to say that the road to Paris was now open and that the battle was lost. Churchill did his best to encourage Reynaud to carry on the fight, but he was under no illusions about the gravity of the situation. He telegraphed his despair to Roosevelt. 'The small countries are simply smashed up one by one, like matchwood. And even Britain expects to be attacked soon, both from the air and by parachute and airborne troops in the near future, and we are getting ready for them.'

On 16 May Churchill flew to Paris to encourage the French to stay in the war. He was confident that the Germans could be beaten, but Reynaud was not convinced: not surprising, given the Germans' swift advance through his country.

On 20 May German armoured columns reached Amiens and pushed on to Abbeville, cutting off the British Expeditionary Force from the French army and leaving hundreds of thousands of British, French and Belgian soldiers trapped, with their backs to the sea. Rommel and Hitler were sure the war would soon be over.

On 26 May the evacuation of Allied troops from Dunkirk began, and that evening Helene Milosevo arrived in a Rolls Royce at the Polish Embassy in Paris. The next day, with her car loaded with food and champagne, Josef gave her directions of where to find Albert, and a note saying that Barbara had given birth to a boy and that mother and child were well.

This news added to Albert's joy at seeing Helene again, and the following three days were like something out of a fairy tale. *'It all seemed so unreal and yet infinitely enjoyable,'* he wrote.

Albert was given leave by his Commanding Officer and Helene set out to make the unexpected break as memorable for him as she could. They found it easy to slip back into each other's lives, and their relaxed natures and deep love meant that, even though they knew they were together only for a brief interval, they could enjoy every second to the full. But three days is not an eternity, and soon it was time for Albert once again to walk out of her life.

'Do you think we will ever meet in more bizarre circumstances?' he asked as he buried his head in her bosom.

'I doubt it, my darling. We can certainly say our times together have never been dull!'

'Where will you go from here?' asked Albert.

'I have no idea. Perhaps soon back to Budapest. I need to sing.'

'I know, but please be careful. Europe is a dangerous place.'

'Have no fear, my darling. Helene Milosevo can look after herself.'

Albert nodded and pulled away. He felt it was time to go, before he started mouthing idiotic things about love. He longed to ask her if she wanted to see him again, longed to know if he featured in her plans for the future, but somehow he knew it was best to keep silent. She had never wanted long-term commitments, and there was no reason why she should have changed. He felt desperately depressed as he raised his hand and turned away, and wondered if this really was the last time he would set eyes on her striking features.

In fact, he had to wait until March 1946 for the answer to this question. By then Hungary was an integral part of the Soviet bloc, and its new leaders were suspicious of Westerners and reluctant to cooperate in any way. After many rebuffs he managed to find out the barest of facts, which told him enough: Helene had been killed in the war, how or where he never found out. His one comfort was that she had been buried in Budapest.

'I cried for three days,' he wrote, 'I should have expected it. After all, I lost most of my friends during the war, and she was the closest.'

By early June, Hitler saw the prize of Paris within his grasp, something that had evaded the Kaiser during four long years of battle between 1914 and 1918, and on 2 June he ordered the first bombing raid on the city. That same day the 1st Polish Division was ordered up to the front, and Albert's long wait was over.

By then the battle for France was reaching its inevitable conclusion. Even Mussolini thought it was safe to declare war on her, a fact that was soon confirmed when, on 10 June, the French were driven back across the Seine and retreated in some disorder towards the Loire. Paul Reynaud and General de Gaulle were coming to the conclusion that their only hope now lay in a final stand in Brittany.

With the outlook growing ever darker, America continued to send words of comfort to Churchill, but not much else, although Roosevelt was assuring him that he would do something with great speed. But the only thing that was going full speed ahead was the German advance, and the only thing of paramount importance to the British at that time was to evacuate any remaining troops they had in France as quickly as possible, and without suffering too many casualties.

Churchill once more found himself urging the French to keep fighting, and he suggested that they make Paris a fortress and fight in every street. Marshal Petain froze with horror and shook his head in disagreement. Nothing would be gained by making Paris a ruin, and soon afterwards he was begging Paul Reynaud to seek an armistice.

Unaware of all this panic and argument, Albert had spent most of the time since he had moved to the battle zone retreating. It was soul-destroying for the Poles, who had hoped that their chance to avenge their country's misery had at last arrived. Instead they saw more of their comrades cut down by the superior force of an enemy full of confidence and self-belief. Albert was convinced that the only troops on the Allied side who could match that belief were the Poles, and they alone could not overcome the great German machine.

He fought with a wild bravado, bolstered by the feeling that, if he died, he would at least have done something worthwhile for his country, and when on the outskirts of Reims a bullet tore through the calf muscle of his left leg and shattered the bone, he was almost disappointed that it had not killed him.

His war was temporarily over, and soon so would be the war in France. By half-past six on the morning of 14 June, German troops had reached the Place de la Concorde and a German command post had been established in the Hôtel Crillon. Two million Parisians had already fled, and those that remained awoke to the sound of German loud-speakers announcing that there would be a curfew that evening starting at 8.00 p.m.

Later that morning, the Germans triumphantly unfurled a huge swastika flag beneath the Arc de Triomphe, and their Fourth Army marched in victory down the Champs-Elysées. Hitler's triumph was nearly complete.

On 15 June the Germans took Verdun, and Reynaud knew that if the Americans did not come into the war 'at a very early date', France would be unable to continue fighting. Churchill, well aware of this, exhorted Roosevelt to enter the war, but this plea was no more successful than the ones that had preceded it, and on the 16th, when the Germans entered Dijon, Marshal Petain, as Deputy Prime Minister, advised the French cabinet to call an immediate armistice.

Paul Reynaud was left no option but to ask Britain to release France from her agreement not to make a separate peace. As a last resort, Churchill offered France an 'Anglo-French Union', which would continue to make war even if France was defeated. Reynaud was the only one of his colleagues to favour the plan, and so immediately resigned.

That evening, Petain, having formed a new government, asked the Germans for an armistice, and on 21 June, in a clearing in the forest of Compiègne, seventy-six kilometres from Paris, came the final French humiliation when she was forced to sign the armistice in the same railway carriage as Marshal Foch had made the Germans sign in 1918.

In less than nine months a sixth nation had succumbed to the mighty German war machine.

Albert was carried into the hospital at Reims just hours before the Germans captured the town. Luckily for him, the doctor who set his shattered leg was well aware that a Polish officer was in grave danger from the Germans once they overran the hospital. Discovering that Albert spoke fluent French, he instructed the nurses to strip him of his bloodstained uniform, and to give him the identity papers of a French officer who had died earlier in the day. Eight hours later when the Germans stormed into the hospital Albert Mieszkowski had become Albert Normand.

Albert realised that his future was now very uncertain. There was no question of him being able to try an escape and so, along with all the other wounded, he could only wait and see what the Germans would do. Their intentions towards anyone unlucky enough not to be French in the hospital soon became apparent, and a few days after it was occupied there were several empty beds belonging to those who could not prove French identity. Albert owed a lot to the quick thinking of the doctor.

It was not until the first week of July that he and his fellow patients learnt what the German Military had in store for them. Once they were deemed fit to move, the Germans were not slow to carry out the armistice agreement that all French prisoners-of-war were to remain under German control, and so, with his leg still in plaster, Albert and the rest of the French soldiers from the hospital were loaded onto cattle trucks and taken to Stalag 3b in Silesia.

Once again Albert had escaped with his life and, although he was under no illusions as to what the future held for him in a camp, he considered himself lucky not to have faced torture or a firing squad. The train journey, to someone who was still weak and in pain, proved arduous, and he had to draw on all his remaining strength to survive. By the time the doors of his cattle truck were opened, there were already those lying on the filthy floor who would not be bothering the guards at Stalag 3b.

Albert's recollection of Stalag 3b lost nothing by the time he was able to tell his family. It was a part of his life that would always be emblazoned on his memory, even though at the time he had done his best to close his mind to the hunger, disease and filth that soon became prevalent in the camp. In constant pain from his leg, once the plaster had been removed – *'at least a month too early'* – there were times when he felt he was not going to survive but, fortified by a strong determination to see his family again, he fought as best he could against bouts of depression and the feeling that really there was not much point in going on living. However, ten months into a captivity that he had resigned himself to lasting for years, a chance to get out suddenly came his way and, still as resourceful as ever, he was not slow to grab it.

Once Petain had formed a French government in Vichy, the Germans announced that they would repatriate all terminally ill French soldiers. Albert, quick to see his opportunity, managed to convince the camp authorities that he was suffering from terminal TB by providing false urine samples bought off a fellow prisoner, and on 3 June 1941, weak but hardly able to believe his luck, he was back in France.

He made for Lyon, with the idea of getting to the south and then into Spain where he hoped he might be able to reach England. It was here, in a little bar off the Place Bellecour, that he learned for the first time the full facts of France's defeat and of Britain's defiance.

'In that man Churchill,' the barman told him with obvious respect, 'Britain has a man to beat the Nazis.'

Albert did not dwell long in Lyon, feeling uneasy about the presence of so many German troops, and moved on to Nîmes. By then, he had been constantly on the move for two weeks, and the condition of his leg was deteriorating alarmingly and he was running a fever. He knew his leg was infected and needed immediate medical treatment, but the question was where and how did he find the right place? Albert was very lucky not to die in Nîmes, but the very seriousness of his condition was his saviour, for on his second night in the town he stumbled semi-conscious and hallucinating into a café, and collapsed onto the floor.

Three days later he regained consciousness in a small hospital run by an Order of nuns in the village of Boucoiran about halfway between Nîmes and Alès.

Over a period of a month, the nuns saved his leg, and nursed him back to something like good health. *'I certainly have two legs only because of their devotion,'* he wrote. *'They were a wonderful Order and their dedication to saving my leg I'm sure came only second to their love of God.'*

Then on 18 July, the Mother Superior paid him her first visit.

'Good morning, Monsieur, I'm glad to see that you are looking a little better and that we have managed to save your leg.'

Albert moved his bad leg under the sheets – the pain had almost gone. 'Thanks to you, Mother Superior, I'm making a fine recovery. My leg feels almost as good as new and I'm altogether much stronger. I was very lucky to have been brought here.'

'Indeed you were, young man. And now that you are nearly fit I have something to tell you.'

She sat down on the side of the bed. 'I don't know if you remember, but you collapsed in a café in Nîmes. Unfortunately, you were shouting your hatred of all Germans in Polish while you lay on the floor. Luckily, not for too long, as a member of the Resistance was drinking at one of the tables and thought quickly. You have him to thank for saving your life. However, Monsieur, it is very difficult for some people to keep their mouths shut, and the Gestapo in Nîmes know that a Polish Officer was in their vicinity, and they are very angry at not having found him. I think by now they have nearly given up any hope and believe that you have been spirited away. However, I need hardly tell you, Monsieur, that they would still very much like to have a talk with you.'

'Dear God, Mother Superior, I must have put your Order in great risk.'

'Oh, the Germans came sniffing around, but you were well hidden by then. We are proving very useful to the Resistance as a 'safe house' now that they are better organised, and they keep us well informed of all enemy movements in this area.'

'Nevertheless, I should go as quickly as I can. They might come back, and I couldn't live with myself if your nuns suffered because of me. After all, I have French papers and the Gestapo have no idea what I look like.'

The Mother Superior shook her head. 'Unfortunately it is not as easy as that. Your papers are out of date for this area. You would soon be picked up and I think you might have a little difficulty persuading them that you are French. Have you a family? Where are they now? Give me the name of your sisters and brothers? Where is your permit? Can you answer questions like that and know that the Germans can verify them?'

Albert held up a hand. 'Enough, I take your point. So what do I do now?'

'Leave it to me.' She laughed as she saw the look of surprise cross Albert's face. 'I may be a servant of God, but already I hate the Nazis. Maybe the Lord would disapprove, Monsieur, but to tell you the truth, I don't ask him.'

Albert lay back against the pillows and relaxed – he felt he was in good hands.

Two days later she brought a man to his room. Paul Jankowski was in his early thirties, about five foot ten inches, stockily built, with short dark hair and enormous hands. His eyes were wide and friendly and glowed with confidence. In 1905, at the age of sixty-three, his grandfather, Alex Jankowski, had moved his family from Poland to Lyon and started a small accountancy business. He died four years later, leaving Paul's father, who in 1906 had married Maria Laport, the daughter of a banker, to run the firm. Paul had been born on 3 May 1907. On the death of his grandfather, his father had moved the business to Alès, acquired a partner, become a naturalised Frenchman, and bought a small chateau a few kilometres from the town. In 1916 he had been fatally wounded in the trenches, leaving the firm to his partner and Paul. Never recovering from this loss, Paul's mother had died a year later. Now Mayor of Alès and active with the Resistance, Paul still lived in the chateau with his wife and fourteen-year-old daughter.

'This is the man who saved you at the café,' said the Mother Superior. 'He is also leader of the Resistance in this area.'

Albert, who was sitting in a chair by the bed, moved to get up.

'No, no,' said Paul. 'Please stay seated. Your leg . . .'

Albert sank back gratefully. He did not admit it too much to the nurses but it still hurt to stand. 'I gather you saved my life and, if I'm not much mistaken, you must be of Polish origin with a name like that.'

'That's correct. My grandfather came to France in 1905. So I understood every word you were saying. You were not being very polite about the Germans!'

'Oh God! I can't remember a thing!'

Paul looked down at Albert. Even though the Mother Superior had told him that he was far from fit, it only took one look at his tall emaciated frame in his ill fitting clothes and his sunken eyes for him to realise that the Mother Superior had understated the situation.

'You want to get to Spain?' he asked.

Albert gave him a weak smile. 'Just as soon as I can. Especially as I'm putting these brave women in danger. Can you help me?'

'Let's see your leg.'

Albert pulled up his trouser. The leg was like a thin stick ready to break at the slightest pressure. The muscles had almost withered away, and there was still some discoloration round the bullet wound.

'You intend to walk across the Pyrenees with that?'

'Why not?'

Paul flashed a look at the Mother Superior. 'I had forgotten what an obstinate breed the Poles are! My father was just the same.'

She smiled and moved across to put a hand on Albert's shoulder. 'I hear they are brave as well.'

'And foolish too,' added Paul.

Albert gazed up at the two people and knew what they were thinking. 'I won't make it?'

'Not a chance,' said Paul bluntly. 'That leg of yours wouldn't carry you on two kilometres of flat ground. The Pyrenees . . . ha, you wouldn't stand a chance, and, what's more, you would put your guide in great danger. They do not come cheap, Monsieur. No, no, if you want to reach Spain you must rest and eat. I'm no doctor but I would say you have no hope of making the journey for at least another two months.'

'But I can't stay here!' cried Albert.

'You don't have to,' replied Paul. 'You can come home with me. You speak excellent French and with new family papers the Nazis will never suspect. You could even be helpful in our organisation. Good young men are hard to come by. Well, what do you say?'

Bitterly disappointed as he was, Albert knew how lucky he was to get such an offer. He wrote: *'I just had to accept the inevitable. This man whom I had only met a few moments ago was offering me a lifeline and a chance to get back into the war against the Nazis, and at the same time remove the danger I was presenting the nuns.'*

'I have little choice, I think. You are right, of course, my leg would not stand up to a long hard walk. If I can stay with you and also be of some help until I'm fit to make the run for Spain, that seems the best solution. However I hope I'm not putting you and your family in danger?'

'There are many more things that put them in greater danger at the moment, Monsieur, I assure you. Once I get you papers you will blend into the background. We will give you a family in Lyon and you have come to stay with your cousins. You can remain safely here, I assure you, until the papers are ready. I will bring the history of the family tomorrow and then you can memorize everything in case you are ever stopped by the Germans.'

'I don't know how to thank you,' said Albert. 'Twice now you have come to my rescue.'

'Think nothing of it. You may well live to regret today! Now, Monsieur, I must leave you. I will return tomorrow afternoon.'

The Mother Superior patted Albert's shoulder. 'A good solution, Monsieur. And one I think will fit your character.' She smiled as she moved to the door with Paul. 'Relax for the next few days and let us do the worrying.'

Sitting in the empty room, Albert could still feel her presence. He would miss her. She had known all along he was not strong enough to make the trip to Spain, but she had held her tongue until she had another alternative to offer him. No doubt she had figured the disappointment would be less. She was right, of course; he wondered if she was ever wrong.

He wrote in his diary. *'I could go on about her for page after page, so clear is my memory of her, and so full is my admiration, but space is limited. She was a tiny little creature wrapped in her robes, and I could only see a small amount of her round cheerful face. The strength that emanated from her was awe-inspiring, and she was full of spirit and brave as a lioness. She had a marvellous gift of seeming to be able to read one's mind and so pour balm on one's troubled thoughts. God indeed had a good servant and I was lucky enough to be at the receiving end of her kindness. In her presence I felt totally inadequate, as I think most of the nuns did as well. That they loved her I have no doubt. I'm sure God forgave her for hating the Nazis. Like Helene, she will always have a special place in my heart.'*

As good as his word, Paul returned the next day with Albert's new identity. 'Albert Fouchard, a twenty-six-year old from Lyon. No sisters or brothers, just you and your mother. Your father is dead. Simple. Anyway, read this and you won't go wrong.'

As Albert took the piece of paper he laughed. 'Soon I will forget who I really am! You are being most kind, and I can't quite see why.'

'Don't worry yourself about it, Monsieur. Let me just say I admire the Poles, and think that a man with such hate in his heart could be a great help against these bloody Nazis. And Albert – if I may call you that – I'm not a pessimist like many of my countrymen. You see, I sense a crack in their armour. Hitler made a bad mistake when he invaded Russia.'

'He has done what!' asked an incredulous Albert. 'Tell me more! I'm obviously very out of touch.'

Paul sat down on the bed – Albert was sitting in the only chair. 'Not content with being the master of eight European capitals, he invaded the Soviet Union on 22 June. A year after that traitor Petain surrendered.'

'My God,' said Albert. 'And Britain?'

'Still fighting. We have a radio now in Alès and we receive many reports from them. Anyway, would you like me to tell you a little more?'

'Yes, please.'

'Hungary and Albania are now at war with the Soviets as well.'

'Oh God! Hungary!'

'A reason?'

'No, not really. I just had a friend once . . . it's nothing, please go on.'

'Now, let me think what else might interest you. The Russians are fighting hard. Hitler no doubt has his eyes on Moscow, but he had better get there before the winter . . . Oh yes, of course, Poland. Nothing of much encouragement there, I'm afraid. Jews go on dying, but then, we hear they are even being killed in Norway and Holland now. It seems anyone wanting to ingratiate themselves to the Germans just has to kill a Jew. Britain is bombing Germany and Churchill continues to make stirring speeches. And Britain is helping the Resistance. But that is another story.'

'Tell me.'

'Very well. At first we were disorganised and we lost many men and some women, but very slowly we are becoming more cunning. The British are sending us more and more help as time goes on. Guns, explosives, radios, and now even men and women to get us into shape. There is some resentment over this – especially amongst the communist group – but they are being short-sighted. In my opinion, we can't do much effectively without help, even if it does mean losing a bit of French pride. We have a good organisation here. United and very pro-British. As you know, I'm the leader. I was made Mayor of Alès last autumn, and this gives me the excuse to travel about a bit more without raising the Gestapo's suspicions. I must say it's different to accountancy! It is dangerous, Monsieur, but most satisfying when we are successful. We killed our first two Gestapo three days ago. There were reprisals, of course, but we must accept that.'

'Reprisals?'

'Three young men shot from the next-door village in front of their families.'

'God. Is it worth it?'

'Of course. We must all be prepared to die for France and freedom.'

Albert swallowed hard. He had been through a lot since the beginning of the war and had grown to accept death, but this man was hard as steel. He knew this was no time for a conscience, but young people . . . and innocent too.

'It must take a resolute man to make such a decision.'

Albert was not surprised by Paul's reply.

'Not really – just a belief in the justness of our cause. Innocents will always die in a war. It is up to us to make sure they do not die in vain.'

Albert had to admit that he was probably right.

'Apart from sabotage and assassinations, our other task,' Paul continued, 'is to get Allied airmen across to Spain. As the British increase their bombing, more and more of them are coming through to us. It is a complicated network, and not yet quite honed to perfection, but it is beginning to work and will get better. When you come to Alès, you will see.'

Chapter 11

On the morning of 25 July 1941 Albert climbed rather painfully onto Paul's motorcycle for the journey to the Chateau. It was a sad moment parting from the Mother Superior and the nuns, but he was relieved that his departure would remove the danger of the Gestapo finding him at the Convent.

The road from Boucoiran to Alès runs for 3½ kilometres beside the river Gard until it meets the river Gardon d'Alès, which flows through the rich plain of the Gardonnenque. A further twenty-two kilometres on up the valley is Alès, a rather dreary town on a bend of the river Gardon. The Mother Superior had told Albert that its one claim to fame was that it had once been a centre for the silk trade, and that Pasteur had come to study the diseases of the silkworms from 1866–68. 'Otherwise, Monsieur, it has nothing at all to recommend it.' As they crossed the Gardon by the Pont de la Prairie and drove into the Boulevard Gambetta, Albert immediately realised what she meant.

Before going to the Chateau, Paul had decided to introduce Albert to Jacques Gregori, who owned a small garage two-thirds of the way along the Boulevard, and who was an important member of the Resistance in the town. He was a rather gruff, middle-aged man of medium height, already growing bald, and with the tell-tale red flecks across his cheeks that told you he liked a drink or two. From the moment they shook hands, Albert felt his animosity.

The introduction complete, Paul took Gregori aside and started to whisper in his ear. It was obvious to Albert by their glances that they were discussing him and whatever was being said was certainly not going down well with Gregori. Albert saw him shake his head vigorously as Paul shrugged and turned back towards him.

He was laughing as he reached him. 'Ah, Jacques is too suspicious – thinks it's wrong for me to trust you. He will come round in time. He is a good man and is right to be on his guard. These are very dangerous times for all of us.'

'Looking back, it was not surprising,' Albert wrote, *'Seeing that I was a Pole and half an invalid. He must have wondered what use I would be to the Resistance, but I think after a few months he grew to trust me. As for myself – well, I could never quite understand the man, and when he got drunk he became very unreliable. I was never happy at knowing that he held my life, and that of Paul's, in his rather shaking hands. In the end, though, he confounded me and I regret now that he never enjoyed my full confidence.'*

Leaving a scowling Gregori behind them, Paul took the motorcycle through the town and back to the river, where they crossed the Pont Lenine and turned right onto the road leading to la Grand-Combe. Seven kilometres out of Alès, they turned right off the road onto a gravel drive that brought them to the front of the Chateau. *'I was very glad we hadn't run into any road blocks,'* wrote Albert. *'Paul had told me there was nothing to worry about as my papers were in order, but even so, it wasn't only the sun that had made me sweat.'*

Annette Jankowski was standing by the front door as Paul came to halt and Albert saw the relief on her face as she ran forward to kiss him.

'You must be the young Pole my husband has been telling me about,' she said, turning to Albert. 'I worry a lot about him at the moment, and especially with a stranger on his bike. There are too many Germans about for me to feel comfortable when Paul is away.'

Albert held out a hand. 'Well, we certainly didn't have any trouble – no road blocks and only a few uninterested soldiers. I suppose they have grown used to seeing the motorcycle. But I would hate to think that I was putting you into further danger.'

'Oh, you're probably right about Paul's machine, and please don't get me wrong, Monsieur, I'm delighted to have you here. In fact, everyone who is against the Germans is welcome in this house. Besides, I hear you are in no fit state to make for Spain. A few months here will soon put the strength back into your leg.'

Albert nodded. Her hand was rough and calloused and she looked tired and undernourished. The strain of her husband's activities was obviously beginning to tell. To put an age on her was impossible; she could easily have been over forty, but at a later date he found out she was only thirty-one. Her long, unkempt hair and hollow features did no justice to a face that at one time must have been very attractive, but she stood tall and straight, and he soon discovered she was a proud woman.

Years later he wrote. '*Hidden beneath her worried expression and total disregard for her looks was an attractive, yes, perhaps even beautiful, face. But Paul worked her too hard, and expected too much – God knows why, for he always seemed to have money. The whole time I was with them I never saw her get help from anyone, except perhaps from the girl who, moments later, came running round the corner of the Chateau. I had never seen a young girl so beautiful, and I stared at her for too long and caused her some embarrassment. I could tell immediately that this was the daughter Paul had told me about, for she had identical features to her mother. The only difference was her age, and work had not yet caught up with her.*

'*Indeed for two whole weeks I kept telling myself that it was because I had been starved of female companionship for so long that I found Eugénie so attractive, especially as she was only fourteen. She had that same presence about her that I had found so attractive in Helene, and as I got to know her better I found she had a maturity that belied her age. I think this was attributable to the war. Forced by circumstance, many young people grew up very quickly in that period. Her personality, however, was not carved out by the war – this was the result, I'm sure, of having two of the most wonderful parents. Although Annette suffered from Paul's meanness with money, I soon learnt of her fortitude, kindness and devotion to her family through a frightening and dangerous period, and this was something that I greatly admired. It left me wishing that one day I would be the same to my family, if I survived the war and was lucky enough to have one.*

'*This wish became stronger and stronger every day that I spent with the Jankowskis, because I found myself falling in love with their young daughter. Her dark hair and blue eyes shone with vitality, and I had no doubt that her budding beauty would blossom as she grew older. At first I tried to hide my feelings – what would my parents have thought of me courting a fourteen-year-old girl! It was wrong, I kept telling myself – I was an oversexed, lustful young man – but I found this was not the case. I did not just wish to release my lust on Eugénie, which, in any case, I feared would ruin a growing friendship that was becoming so important to me. Oh yes, I desired her – but I found that I could wait, for of one thing I was sure – at some stage I would marry her. Looking back on my life it seems extraordinary to me that, with Helene, I was so certain our relationship would never last, but with Eugénie, I knew beyond all doubt, at a very early stage in our relationship, that one day we would be man and wife. I have never been able to explain it.'*

At five minutes to eight on the morning of 7 December 1941, three hundred and sixty-six Japanese planes struck at Pearl Harbour. On the same day, they bombed three American Pacific Islands, Guam, Wake and Midway, and 24,000 of their troops were on the way to the Malayan Peninsula. America was at war with Japan.

A day later, Singapore and Kai Tak airport on Hong Kong were attacked by Japanese planes. In London the news cast a pall of depression over Churchill's cabinet, and he wondered if Roosevelt would now ever commit himself to fighting the Germans.

Hitler was overjoyed. 'With Japan as an ally we cannot lose the war. They have never been vanquished in three thousand years,' and on 11 December he declared war on America. It was perhaps his greatest error, and certainly the single most decisive act of the war. The last thing Roosevelt wanted was a war against Germany when he was facing a struggle in the Pacific against enormous odds. To him and to the American people, Europe was half a globe away. Eventually, however, it was to ensure the overthrow of Hitler for, whatever his commitment to the war in the Pacific, Roosevelt poured first ships, then planes, and finally troops, into Europe, which slowly tipped the balance in favour of the Allies.

On Christmas Day, Hong Kong surrendered, and 11,000 British soldiers were taken prisoner. On the same day, on the other side of the world in Leningrad, 3,700 people died of starvation. It was the end of a bad year for the Allies, and Hitler told a group of friends that he hoped 1942 would prove to be as successful.

Throughout German-occupied Europe, however, there was growing a belief that eventually Germany would be defeated, and nothing bolstered this mood of guarded optimism more than the activities of the various Resistance groups scattered about Europe, and the continual arrival from England of men to join them behind enemy lines, or the news coming from England, over the clandestine radios, that America was now at war with Hitler and that his army was in retreat in Russia.

In January of the New Year, Jean Moulin, the ex-Mayor of Chartres, who had escaped to England, parachuted back into France and began to try unifying the various factions of the Resistance and to coordinate action, and Albert finally abandoned any idea of trying to get to England since by then he was an integral part of the Alès/Nîmes Resistance. Added to this, the pull of Eugénie, and the pain in his leg that still at times kept him awake at night, persuaded him he could be more use in France, especially as they were now involved in the running of one of the main escape routes for Allied airmen, known as the 'Comet line'. The Chateau had become one of the 'safe houses' where the airmen were hidden until they could continue their journey across France and over the Pyrenees to Spain.

Albert had to admit that he enjoyed the danger and the chance to play an active part in something so successful. *'The constant danger and knowledge that capture meant torture and certain death was like a drug to me. I was almost ashamed of voicing my feelings to anyone, but one day I told Paul and he confessed that he was the same. I had often wondered what had made him stay in France – he could so easily have slipped away with his family to Switzerland or Spain as soon as Hitler invaded his country, but now I knew. He had been bored before the war with his accountancy, and the Resistance had given him the chance to enjoy the excitement of real and terrifying danger. We both must have been a little mad to enjoy risking our lives, but this was a fact, and not until things started to go badly wrong did the drug lose its power.'*

However successful they were, and however much the adrenalin flowed, Albert never shook off the dull pain in his stomach whenever he heard of the terrible suffering still being borne by the citizens of Poland. News was sporadic, but every now and then, the hidden radios picked up horror stories of more German brutality to the Jews, and of thousands of deaths practically every day. Rumour was strong that at Auschwitz a death camp had been set up, and the Resistance in Lyon had discovered a camp at Recebedou in the Pyrenees which they strongly suspected was a holding camp for eventual deportation. Albert realised it was not only the Polish Jews that were suffering.

The message was loud and clear – the mass killings were continuing in an effort to carry out Hitler's 'Final Solution'.

The constant killings in Poland and western Russia had horrified the Allied governments, including those exiles on whose land most of the tyranny was taking place, and at a meeting in London, nine occupied countries signed a declaration that all those guilty of 'war crimes' would be punished after the war. Albert heard with particular pleasure that General Sikorski had signed for Poland.

This news did not ease the immediate pain, which went very deep, and even his growing involvement with Eugénie could not stem the constant flow of grief. He wrote: *'I knew she could not understand and I was reluctant to burden one so young with such a very personal pain. But her very presence helped me to control my grief and see a brighter future round the corner. Every day she had grown more important to me.'*

By February, the Resistance was on the whole in good shape and on the evening of the 15th some of Paul's group crept into Gregori's garage to celebrate the news that another four airmen had arrived safely in Spain. It was their practice at these meetings to listen to London on the radio that Gregori had hidden in his workshop. They were in high spirits, from a little too much cognac, as he fiddled with the buttons, but as the voice of Churchill filled the cold air the laughter died away and they huddled round the set. When he announced that Singapore had fallen, the whole atmosphere in the room changed and everyone exchanged worried glances.

'Here is the moment to display the calm and poise, combined with grim determination,' Churchill said, 'which not so long ago brought us out of the very jaws of death. The only real danger would be a weakening in our purpose, and therefore in our unity –that is the mortal crime. Whoever is guilty of such a crime, or of bringing it about to others, should have a millstone hung round his neck and be cast into the sea. Do not despair, we must remember that we are no longer alone. We are in the midst of a great company. Three-quarters of the human race are now moving with us. The whole future of mankind may depend upon our action and upon our conduct. So far we have not failed. We shall not fail now. Let us move forward steadfastly together into the storm, and through the storm.'

Gregori switched off the radio. *'We just looked at each other,'* wrote Albert, *'and realised that Britain was once again facing a crisis. We all knew what Singapore meant to her. No one spoke or moved for several minutes after the radio went quiet.'*

'It is fortunate for us all that Britain has Churchill,' said Gregori, breaking the silence.

'And we have General de Gaulle and the resolve to win,' replied Paul.

Everyone's head nodded in agreement and, without another word being spoken, the meeting broke up and Paul and Albert climbed onto the motorcycle and drove back to the Chateau. As he dismounted by the front door Paul grabbed Albert's arm. *'His grip was firm – almost urgent,'* remembered Albert.

'When we do win, will you ask me for my daughter's hand?'

'I couldn't see Paul's face in the dark,' wrote Albert, *'and I thought it a funny time to ask me such a question, but his tone was very friendly. By now I had learnt that he was a plain-speaking man. Blunt to the point of almost seeming rude. I had also learnt that he liked simple straight*

answers to his questions. 'Perhaps I won't be able to wait that long!' I replied.'

For the remainder of 1942, the 'Comet Line' continued passing Allied airmen down the line and the Chateau was seldom empty. For Albert it was a mixed year. Happy with Eugénie one minute, terrified the next, as he escorted an Allied airman from the Chateau, and deeply depressed as news of even more atrocities in Poland filtered through to him. Terrible reports were coming out of Warsaw where the Germans were rounding up thousands of Jews and sending them to the village of Treblinka. Rumours were rife that over a quarter of a million Jews had been slaughtered there in seven weeks. *'Of course, at the time I could not confirm this,'* wrote Albert, *'and for my own peace of mind I tried not to believe it. Now I know it to be true, and it is well known that it was the largest and swiftest slaughter of a single community, Jewish or non-Jewish, in the war. My God! How my heart still bleeds for all those poor people!'*

At times, he felt like leaving the Chateau, to work his way back to Poland and join one of the partisan groups, but each time he realised the folly of his intention before it was too late. *'Anyway, each time the thought passed through my mind, I knew that really I owed my allegiance to Paul, and that I shouldn't desert either him or Eugénie.'*

Then Annette tried to put pressure on him to give up his dangerous work, and take Eugénie somewhere safer than the Chateau, so convinced was she that sooner or later their luck would run out. *'I knew I was letting her down by refusing, but how could I leave Paul and Gregori when they needed me so badly? The chain of command was so important, and we each had a separate job to do. If we lost anyone, it took weeks to train someone else, and you never knew that you weren't taking on a traitor.'*

Elsewhere in Europe, the Allies were tasting their first successes, and in Russia, the Germans were taking heavy casualties as their forces were forced to retreat. As 1942 drew to a close, the Axis powers were in retreat in Libya, in New Guinea, at Stalingrad and in the Caucasus. But the war was by no means won, as hundreds of millions of captive people went into 1943 still under the control of the Axis powers.

During the first week of January 1943 Paul and Annette agreed that Eugénie and Albert could get married that summer, once she had reached the age of sixteen. Although they were concerned about her age, the constant danger of one of them being picked up by the Gestapo and so leading to them all being arrested, was never far from their thoughts;

so why shouldn't she enjoy some happiness while she was healthy and free?

As if their reasoning needed any confirmation, 15 January saw the first arrests of members of the 'Comet Line' in Brussels by the Gestapo. Paul had always said to Albert that a line of such length and involving so many people – it ran from Brussels, Holland and France to the Pyrenees – was one day bound to be betrayed.

Once the first arrests were made, more followed each day, spanning all three countries. In a very short space of time, several hundred of those who had helped to organise or guard the escape route were in the hands of the Gestapo. Many did not survive, and the 'Comet Line' was severely mauled. However, it had done a marvellous job, and hundreds of Allied airmen owed their freedom to the brave men and women who defied all the odds to get them to Spain.

The Jankowskis sat and held their breath. All movement of airmen had to be suspended. Albert remembered the tension. *'They were greatly upset by the setback, and lived in terror of the Gestapo. They were convinced that it was only a matter of time before they would be dead. Even the news that, on 24 April, the Resistance had assassinated Paul Gassovski, one of the hated organisers of the Malice in Marseille, failed to cheer them up.'*

However, in early May, they were still free, and had begun to believe that they might survive. 'Our security must have been better than I thought,' Paul said to Albert. 'Or those arrested must have been very brave.'

For many of their compatriots were already dead, and most had been hideously tortured. Some they knew, some they had never seen. Others, like themselves, were lucky – some lived in Lyon, some in Brussels, others in Amsterdam – there was no pattern – no obvious hero who had not cracked under torture. It had to be put down to luck.

So the Jankowskis, and those that were left, set to work slowly and painstakingly putting the 'Line' together again. Their motivation was revenge for their dead comrades, and the belief that every airman saved put another nail in Hitler's coffin. It was even more dangerous work now. The Gestapo were alert, the informers everywhere. With care, and brilliant planning, Paul, Gregori and Albert reactivated the Alès-Montpelier-Pyrenees run. It was tough on the nerves and the risks were enormous, but they were brave men and no quitters, and by the third week of May, they had made their part of the 'Line' operational again. Three days later the first airmen passed safely through their area and on to safety in Spain.

'Paul dug out from the Chateau cellars a bottle of Veuve Clicquot and we drank to our success,' wrote Albert,*' But I had to confess to not getting*

the same buzz from the danger. I think the arrests and deaths had brought home to me, for the first time, how big a risk Paul and I were taking with our women's lives. I'd had time to think of what would happen to Eugénie if the Gestapo ever got their hands on her. It was a new ghost come to haunt me.'

On 3 June, Paul attended a secret meeting in Paris along with thirteen other Resistance leaders representing eight separate movements, during which Jean Moulin successfully managed to persuade them to accept the overall leadership of General de Gaulle, and when he returned he told Albert, 'It was a great day, seeing so many factions all ready to fight under one banner for the freedom of France.'

His joy was to be short lived, for on 7 June, final disaster struck the 'Comet Line', when five English airmen and one American were arrested in Paris as they were being met by two members of the line, Frederic de Jongh and Robert Ayle, both well known to Paul. They were betrayed by Jacques Desoubrie, a young twenty-two-year-old Frenchman (recently recruited by Gregori), who went on to be responsible for the arrest of fifty French and Belgian members of the Resistance, almost all of whom died at the hands of the Gestapo. When, a month later, Jean Moulin was arrested in Lyon and tortured for eleven days before dying, Paul and Gregori resigned themselves to the inevitable end of the 'Comet Line'.

'We have lost too many friends,' Paul cried to Albert. 'Perhaps once all my grief has gone I will start killing Germans again, but at this moment I need a rest. I have no more stomach for the fear and killing, so cheer me up, young Albert, and marry Eugénie.'

On 12 July, two months after her sixteenth birthday, Albert and Eugénie were quietly married using Albert's correct name. 'You are now a Mieszkowski,' he whispered to her that night, as for the first time he felt her soft skin against his.

'And I'm proud to be married to a Pole,' she whispered back.

'I think she really meant it,' he wrote. *'I was certainly proud to be married to her.'*

Four days after their wedding, Albert took Eugénie to meet the Mother Superior, and even though it was nearly three years before he could continue with his diary he wrote: *'I will never forget her look of disapproval as I introduced Eugénie. The smile was still there, and I knew she was not really angry. She congratulated us both and gave Eugénie a Bible. "So young, so young," she kept saying. We talked about America coming into the European war, about the Gestapo who now paid her regular visits, which had forced her to abandon being a "safe house", and about what she hoped the world would be like after the war. "Above all, Monsieur," I remember her saying, "Look after this child and make her happy. No one of her age should have witnessed so much death and unhappiness." We stayed for an hour – I was only to see her three more times. Five months later, on 29 November, she died. Not killed directly by the Germans, but certainly pushed by the pressure and harassment, which hurried her to the grave. Once again I had lost a friend.'*

Albert did not heed the Mother Superior's words, for with Paul, and to a lesser extent Gregori, still suffering from the shock of losing the 'Line' and nearly half of its operatives, he found he was urgently needed for the ever-increasing acts of sabotage. Well aware he was once again putting the women's lives at risk, he nevertheless felt it was his duty to continue, and nothing that Paul and Annette said to him could change his mind. 'I always said the Poles were an obstinate nation,' said Paul ruefully. 'In fact, if my memory serves me right, it was the first thing I said to you in the Convent. I see you have not changed!'

Chapter 12

During the late summer and autumn the Allied successes continued, and on 13 October the new Italian government, having overthrown Mussolini, declared war on Germany, and Italian soldiers joined the Allied forces in trying to break through to Rome.

Meanwhile, in Poland, the subjugation and terrorising of the population continued. On 25 October at Auschwitz, 2,500 Jewish women and girls, who had been locked into a barrack room for three days without any water or food, were dragged out and taken to the gas chamber.

During November at the Majdanek concentration camp, near Lublin, 45,000 survivors of the Warsaw ghetto were machine-gunned in ditches behind the gas chambers, 18,000 of them in a single day. In Lublin itself, 5,000 Jewish soldiers of the Polish army were shot during the last week of the month.

On 3 December in Warsaw, the SS and Gestapo publicly executed a hundred municipal tramway workers as reprisals against recent acts of sabotage, and on 14 December, nine members of the Polish Communist Party were taken out of their prison at Herby and shot.

In Germany that December, the Allied air raids intensified on Berlin, with heavy losses of Allied airmen, and on Christmas Day Roosevelt warned America, 'The war is now reaching the stage when we shall have to look forward to large casualty lists – dead, wounded and missing. War entails just that. There is no easy road to victory, and the end is not yet in sight.'

All too well aware that the war was far from won, and that they were still in grave danger, the arrival of 1944 was welcomed with subdued celebrations by those at the Chateau, although there was an under-current of optimism. There was no doubt the Germans were in trouble and the

Resistance in France, and other partisan groups in the rest of Europe, had scored many successes in the last twelve months. As Paul said, as midnight struck, 'By some miracle we are still alive and, God willing, we can now look forward to the eventual defeat of Nazism. My one regret is that we can no longer help those brave young men who are pounding the German cities from the air.'

The truth was, he was beginning to miss the excitement. *'I had a suspicion that night, as I lay by Eugénie, that soon his self-imposed retirement would come to an end,'* wrote Albert. *'I felt that perhaps, if this was going to be the case, I would be able to spend a little more time with Eugénie. For it had dawned on me that I should have known and understood her better. Looking back on it now, I should have taken more trouble to reassure one so young how much I loved her. I think – no, that is a lie – I bloody well know I failed in that respect.'*

A week later Paul and Gregori travelled to Lyon to make contact with another resistance group who were actively escorting Allied airmen to Spain. They arrived in the city on 9 January, and by sheer bad luck, that evening, two German soldiers were shot dead by the group. The Gestapo's reaction was swift and ruthless, raiding, within two hours of the soldiers' deaths, the house where Paul and Gregori had just arrived. Unknown to them it had been under surveillance for some time. In the battle that ensued, Gregori was captured, along with three men and one woman. Two more men were shot dead, and Paul managed to escape with two other women.

The result was horrifying. The next morning the Germans shot twenty-two French prisoners held in Lyon prison, and the Gestapo brought Gregori back to Alès. On 11 January, an exhausted Paul arrived back at the Chateau, and the next day the Gestapo dragged Gregori's wife and two young sons out of their house, and shot them in front of him. They then took him back to their headquarters where they subjected him to terrible torture before shooting him.

Once again, the Jankowskis were sure they only had hours before they, too, were subjected to the same fate. *'But Jacques Gregori had not cracked,'* wrote Albert. *'He betrayed no one. A drunkard he may have been but, by God, I had misjudged his bravery and loyalty to the cause, Paul and myself. A true patriot had been taken from us.*

'His death hit us all very hard, especially Paul who was suffering fearful guilt at having escaped from Lyon. It was as much as Annette and I could do to stop him committing certain suicide by going into Alès to hunt out any member of the Gestapo he could find. Although he did eventually calm down, and accept that he was not to blame for Gregori's death, he

was never the same man again, growing moody and tending to drink far more than was good for him. This led to him taking risks that he would never have dreamt of taking before Gregori's death, by talking too loudly in the cafés about his hatred of the Germans, and how he wished they could all be made to suffer like Gregori. He became a security risk to the Resistance, and I was convinced he was slipping towards inevitable exposure to the Gestapo either from his own stupidity, or from others who thought he would be safer out of the way. I remember just hoping that the Allies would get to Alès first or once more I risked losing a friend.'

Albert had every right to think that his hope might not be long in coming, for at the end of January, the 880 day siege of Leningrad ended, and the Red Army doggedly, and at great loss of life, continued to push the Germans back; and the Allies had landed at Anzio. Above all else, rumours started to spread amongst the Resistance that an invasion of France would not be long in coming.

In February, Poland saw Stalin's army driving the Germans from the towns and villages in the east, which he then claimed as Soviet territory, while Churchill was busy trying to persuade the Poles in England to give up their claims to Polish sovereignty over this part of their country. His reasoning was that the Poles had secured this piece of land in 1921, under the treaty of Riga after their victory in the Polish-Soviet war, and therefore it was really Soviet territory. However, he stood by the legitimacy of their claim in official correspondence with Stalin, who was already supporting the claims of the Communist-run Polish National Council, based in Russia, to be the post-war Government of Poland. This council had already accepted that eastern Poland was part of the Soviet Union. Elsewhere, the Allies were being massively victorious – on the eastern front, after a setback at Anzio, and in the Pacific.

At the end of February, Eugénie informed Albert she was pregnant. His joy would have overwhelmed him, had he not been so worried about Paul.

In March, British bombers struck at Hamburg, and American bombers struck at the German submarine yards at Vegesack, near Bremen, and on 27 March, Churchill telegraphed to Stalin that the Royal Air Force had 'flung 1,050 tons of explosives on Berlin in 50 minutes. The sky was clear over the target and the raid was highly successful. This is the best Berlin has yet got. Our loss is nine only.'

In April, the fearsome Allied bombing on Germany continued unabated and France waited breathlessly for the invasion, but Albert knew that no one in the Resistance was safe until the Germans were no longer a force to be reckoned with. This they quickly proved they still were, by turning their full fury on the Resistance, as their defeats on the battle field increased. Towards the end of the month, news came through that six German regiments, in the first week, had launched a sweep against the Resistance in the hills around Gex and Oyonnax and in the Jura mountains, killing at least five members and taking over fifteen prisoners. No sooner was Albert digesting this report, than he heard that German agents had captured twenty of the Resistance in Angers. *'I thought then that time was running out. Could our luck hold out?'*

The answer to his question seemed even more unlikely as May saw the Germans publicly hang ninety-nine Resistance fighters in the Auvergne. For the Germans, it was like trying to bring down a brick wall with a nail file, as British Intelligence had by then identified 35,000 active members, region by region, and was sending them regular supplies of arms in preparation for a general uprising. In the face of such a determined enemy, any successes the Germans had were a mere pin-prick in the side of the organisation, however tragic they seemed at the time.

On 4 June, Rome fell to the Americans, and Churchill telegraphed to Roosevelt, 'How magnificently your troops have fought.' Although it was a great morale booster for the hard-pressed Resistance, it was nothing to the news that arrived at the Chateau on 6 June. *'It is a day I will never forget,'* wrote Albert. *'My hand shakes even now as I write. The invasion had begun! At last I knew it could not be long before Germany was forced to retreat, and my child would be brought up in a free country. I remember screaming with joy, yes, screaming, as I ran to find Eugénie. The only thing that slightly spoilt my joy was the thought that I might not be able to bring up my child at Mieszki Wielkie.'*

By dawn on 6 June, eighteen thousand British and American parachutists were on the ground in Normandy and disrupting German lines of communication. By midnight, 155,000 Allied troops were already ashore, and the beachheads were being held.

On 8 June, Stalin telegraphed Churchill, 'Operation Overlord is a source of joy to us all.' And he promised to launch his summer offensive as soon as he could.

At the Chateau the celebrations went on for days, the large sitting room never empty, with people coming up from Alès to shake Paul's hand, and there was a general air of excitement and anticipation as they drank his cognac. Beneath the outward joy, however, there lurked a fear in all their hearts that the Germans might, even at the last hour, push the Allies back into the Channel. And could the Russians go on taking such heavy casualties? Rumour was rife that the losses amongst their young men were colossal, and it proved that the Germans were brave and stubborn fighters. Might not they be able to turn the tide in Normandy as well? No one was in the mood to voice these fears aloud – they just thought about them when they were alone, or nervously discussed them with the family over the kitchen table.

One who was not afraid to air his concern was Paul, especially when, only days after the invasion, on 10 June, in the village of Oradour-sur-Glane, twenty-two kilometres from Limoges, the SS murdered nearly the entire population, including 190 children, as a reprisal for a Resistance attack on a military convoy moving towards the Normandy beachhead. From this cowardly attack only two villagers escaped.

Paul shook his head sadly. 'By God, they are still dangerous – the sting has not yet been removed from their tails. Now they are trapped, they will fight back with ever-increasing ferocity.'

'*I knew he was right,*' wrote Albert. '*I had seen a lot more SS and Gestapo in Alès since the invasion. I felt very ill at ease, especially as Paul was Mayor, and therefore had a very high profile, and I just couldn't get it out of my head that the Gestapo must have suspected him of belonging to the Resistance. It was a time for us to keep our heads down.*'

Paul, however, had other ideas. 'We must rattle them, keep at them constantly, and cause sabotage whenever we can. That way, we will be helping the Allied cause.'

Reluctantly, Albert was drawn into more and more risky acts of sabotage, as the targets got bigger, and thus better guarded. Every time they left the Chateau for another attack, he was sure he would never see Eugénie again. '*Frankly, I couldn't understand how Paul's nerves could take the pressure. I know mine were shot to pieces after a month, and as for poor Eugénie and Annette, God only knew what sort of hell they were going through. Eugénie was wonderful, never once asking me to stop, but she must have wondered if her baby was ever going to have a father to play with.*'

Then in July, just to make matters worse, a coded message was sent to all Resistance groups from General de Gaulle asking them to intensify their attacks on Gestapo troops and known collaborators.

This was grist to the mill for Paul and he immediately put together a list of known informers in the area. Leaving Albert and most of his group to carry on with the sabotage, Paul formed a small special force of dedicated men to carry out assassinations of those that he saw as no better than the lowest form of animal. For five weeks he and four other men went about their task with a ruthlessness that shocked even the hardened men of the Resistance.

On 25 July, another tragedy was unfolding in Poland. In Warsaw, the Polish Home Army, as they called themselves, loyal to the Government-in-exile in London, had decided it was time to throw off the German yoke, before the Red army arrived and took over the city. 'We are ready to fight for the liberation of Warsaw at any moment,' their leader, Lieutenant General Tadeusz Bor-Komorowski, telegraphed to London. 'Be prepared to bomb the airfields at our request. I will announce the beginning of the fight.' The following day the forces hiding in Warsaw were warned to expect the fighting to start any day.

On 1 August, in spite of their London-based government-in-exile advising against it, the Polish Home Army, the People's Army, and armed civilians, making in all 42,500 men and women, rose in revolt against the Germans, determined to liberate the city before the Soviet troops crossed the Vistula. By 2 August they had seized two-thirds of Warsaw, but had not managed to expel the German forces from a crucial east-west axis running between the older part of the city to the north, and the large area of suburbs to the south, which meant they had failed to take the airport, the main station, or any of the Vistula bridges. But they had run out of steam, so all they could do was dig in and defend themselves and hope the Allies came to their aid. They waited three long days for a German counter-attack, and by that time they were confident they could hold it off.

As Warsaw rose in revolt, the Germans were on the retreat everywhere – in Normandy, on the Eastern Front and in Italy. But they were not prepared to give up Warsaw to the insurgents. 'Destroy them by the tens of thousands!' ranted Himmler. It did not take long for his orders to be obeyed. In the third of Warsaw that they still held the Germans entered a hospital and, having killed the head doctor, shot all the patients.

On 4 August, as the expected German counter-attack began, the insurgents appealed for Allied help. Churchill telegraphed to Stalin, 'We are dropping, subject to weather, about 60 tons of equipment and ammunition into the south-west quarter of Warsaw. They are being attacked by one and a half German divisions.' Stalin's reply was blunt and grim. The Soviet Union would not help the insurgents. 'I think that the information that has been communicated to you by the Poles is greatly exaggerated and does not inspire confidence. The Home Army consists of a few detachments, not divisions. They have neither artillery, aircraft or tanks. I cannot imagine how such detachments can capture Warsaw, given the strength of the German forces, including the Hermann Goering division.'

In fact, Stalin had a very good reason for not helping the Poles in Warsaw, as the insurgents were led by men who thought Poland should control its own future as a sovereign state. This was not Stalin's intention, and he knew that sooner or later, this leadership would have to be eliminated, but this would not be easy with a fully mobilised army behind them. It was, therefore, something of a godsend to him, that the Germans would do the dirty work for him, and so he held his advancing army back from the outskirts of Warsaw and sat and waited. He could claim complete innocence, while reaping the fruits of a crime which he would otherwise have to commit at some future date.

On the night that the German counter-attack began, 13 British bombers flew from Foggia in southern Italy to central Poland, which lay at the extreme limit of their range. Five out of thirteen failed to return. Only two got as far as Warsaw, where they dropped twenty-four containers of arms and ammunition. Twelve containers reached the Poles, the other twelve fell into German hands.

On 5 August, German bombers flew over the suburb of Wola and dropped high-explosive and incendiary bombs and, later that day, the insurgents liberated a German forced labour camp near the ruins of the former ghetto, freeing 348 Jews, who immediately joined the uprising.

By 5 August more than 15,000 Polish civilians had been murdered. Worried by this slaughter, the German commander sent out an order forbidding the killing of any more women and children, but the killing of men continued, irrespective of whether they were insurgents or not. Nor did all the units under German command obey the order, and in the suburbs of Wola and Ochota, rape, murder and torture continued of all the population. In three days of slaughter, a further 30,000 civilians were killed.

On the tenth day of their fight against the Germans, the insurgents sent another appeal to Churchill. 'We are conducting a bloody fight,' the message read. 'Warsaw is cut by three routes. Each route is held by German tanks, and the buildings along them burned out. Two German armoured trains on the city's periphery, and artillery from the Praga suburb on the east bank of the Vistula, fire continuously on the town, and are supported by the Luftwaffe.' The message went on to note that only 'one small drop' had come from the Allies. 'On the German-Russian front, silence since the 3rd. We are therefore without any material or moral support. The soldiers and the population look hopelessly at the skies, expecting help from the Allies, but they see only German aircraft. They are surprised, feel deeply depressed, and begin to revile.'

Churchill, well aware of how Britain and France had failed to come to Poland's aid in 1939, immediately sent a message to Stalin asking him if the Allies could use some of his airfields that were only ten to fifteen minutes flying time away from Warsaw. 'They implore machine guns and ammunition. Can you not give them some further help, as the distance from Italy is so great?' He was determined to help if he could and, not waiting for Stalin's reply, authorised the despatch, two nights later, of twenty bombers from Foggia. In fact, twenty-eight bombers set out, of which fourteen reached Warsaw. Three were shot down over the city, and of the thirty-five tons of ammunition and equipment carried, only five tons reached the insurgents.

The Americans were not helpful either, feeling that the Soviets were much better placed to rescue the insurgents than any of the other Allies, as daylight operations were not feasible, and they could only consider 'the minimum of night effort', because of all their other commitments.

In Moscow, on 15 August, the British and American Ambassadors went to the Soviet Foreign Ministry to seek more help for the Warsaw uprising. They were bluntly told that the Soviets considered the uprising 'an ill-advised and not a serious matter, and that the future course of the war would not at all be influenced by it.' That night, a further mission was flown from Foggia. Ten bombers set off, only two returned.

On 18 August, the Communist-controlled National Council in Poland declared Lublin the temporary capital, and in Warsaw the insurgents fought on with growing desperation. Churchill telegraphed Roosevelt, 'The refusal of the Soviets to allow us to use their airfields to bring succour to the insurgents, added to their complete neglect to fly in supplies of their own when only a few score miles away, constitutes an episode of profound and far reaching gravity. If, as is almost certain, the German triumph in Warsaw is followed by wholesale massacre, no measure can be put on the full consequences that will arise.'

Stalin continued to refuse his airfields and the Allies were forced to send what little aid they could from Foggia at night.

After three weeks and four days, the insurgents were still fighting. Churchill, in desperation, made another appeal to Stalin, pointing out that the uprising had been repeatedly called for by Radio Moscow, and that he feared Hitler's cruelties would not end with the insurgents' resistance. 'On the contrary, it seems probable that that is the time when they will begin with full ferocity. The massacre in Warsaw will undoubtedly be a very great annoyance to us when we all meet at the end of the war. Unless you directly forbid it, therefore, we propose to send the planes.'

To use the airfields without Stalin's permission was too much for the Americans, and Roosevelt rejected Churchill's suggestion.

Thus it was over the aid to Warsaw that the Anglo-American unity was broken. Britain was on her own if she wished to defy Stalin, and that would greatly annoy the Soviet leader. When, on 28 August, the advancing Red Army started arresting elements of the Polish Home Army, the future of Poland became the principle cause of contention between the Allies.

On 2 September, the insurgents were forced to abandon more of their positions in the old part of Warsaw and descend to the sewers, but even though they had been forced to withdraw, Churchill still hoped to be able to drop them more supplies wherever they were holding out. Once again, he received no help from the Americans. Roosevelt wrote to him. 'I am informed by my Office of Military Intelligence that the fighting Poles have departed from Warsaw and that the Germans are now in full control. The problem of relief for the Poles in Warsaw has therefore unfortunately been solved by delay and by German action, and there now appears to be nothing we can do to assist them.'

Then suddenly, on 9 September, Stalin had a change of heart and finally informed the Allies that they could use his airfields. Even more surprisingly, he started sending aid to the insurgents. By then, he knew it was far too late – the battle was all but over – the Germans had done his dirty work. It was nothing but a cruel and cynical gesture devised to try and appease Churchill.

On 14 September, the Soviet Army reached the Warsaw suburb of Praga, across the river from the suburbs in which the insurgents were fighting their last heroic, but hopeless, battle.

On 20 September, Polish volunteers flew twenty aircraft from Foggia across the Adriatic, Hungary, Slovakia and Southern Poland in the last attempt to drop supplies to a small group of insurgents, still holding out in woods ten miles west of the city. Five of the twenty were shot down.

On 27 September, the last insurgents surrendered to the Germans, and during the next five days a terrible vengeance was wrought on all who had been captured. During the fighting itself, fifteen thousand Polish resistance fighters had been killed, for a cost of at least 10,000 Germans. In savage reprisals, both during the fighting and after it, an estimated 200,000 Polish civilians had been killed.

After the war, when Albert learnt most of the facts, he was tempted to draw a similarity with the German invasion of Poland in 1939. He wrote in his diary. *'Britain and France held their heads in shame then, and said they should have done more. That they learnt damn all is crystal clear from what happened in Warsaw in 1944. Ashamed once more they may have been, but the truth is, that once again, Polish people had been sacrificed to the dubious necessity for Allied unity. Today we can see where that has got us! I lost many friends in the fighting – two whole families of whom there is no trace. May God forgive those who wouldn't come to Warsaw's aid.'*

In France, events were moving swiftly. On 17 August, the German army and the Gestapo began to flee from Paris. On the 23rd, a French armoured division moved towards the city, entering from the south through the Porte d'Orléans on the 24th. Although there were still pockets of German resistance left, and some civilians were killed in the crossfire, the bells of Paris rang out their victory peals, and finally General de Gaulle walked in triumph down the Champs Elysées on the 26 August.

Albert's joy at this news was tempered by the increased activity of the SS and Gestapo in the Nîmes-Alès area, trying to catch the band that was causing them so many casualties. *'For even if you didn't approve of Paul's methods,'* wrote Albert, *'you had to admire his guts, and his success rate – but I think we all knew it couldn't last.'*

Almost inevitably, Paul's luck ran out on 12 September, when he was arrested as he was trying to make his way back from Nîmes to the Chateau, having killed a young man whom the Resistance knew had been helping the Germans for some time. It had made no difference to Paul and his group that the young man's parents had been held in Lyon prison for two years, and probably were only alive because he had agreed to cooperate with the SS and Gestapo.

Albert received the news at eleven that night, and by 2.00 a.m. on 13 September, he had moved Annette and Eugénie to the relative safety of the Convent, where he was greeted with open arms by the new Mother Superior. *'Our reception was as I had expected from this extraordinary Order. Nothing seemed to frighten them. The new Mother Superior was as brave and contemptuous of the Nazis as her predecessor.'*

At 8.00 p.m. the same day, the SS raided the Chateau. Then they moved into Alès and searched until it was dark. At midnight they arrived at the Convent, and two hours later left empty-handed.

'We lay under the altar of their little chapel so close to each other that we could smell each other's fear,' wrote Albert. *'I heard the SS come into the chapel and listened horrified as they shouted threats and broke up pews and smashed one of the priceless stained glass windows. All through this, I could hear the Mother Superior calmly assuring them that she would never harbour enemies of the Reich. What a woman she turned out to be!'*

On 15 September two German soldiers were shot dead in Alès, where Paul, along with six other men, was being held by the Gestapo. In reprisal he and the six were taken out the next morning and shot. That evening Annette was told the news.

'It was the end of a brave man,' wrote Albert. *'The only thing wrong with him was that he felt he had to win the war on his own. The war in France was nearly over, and if only he had been more patient he would probably be alive today. His death numbed the three of us but, without a doubt, the worst torture was that Annette never got his body back.'*

Nowhere was safe for them now; the Chateau was under twenty-four hour surveillance, and although at times Albert risked going out at night to Alès, he made sure he was back at the Convent by dawn. His work for the Resistance was finished. All he could do was remain cooped up with Annette and Eugénie in the Convent, and hope that the Allies arrived before the Germans found them.

By the end of September the liberation of France was nearly complete. In Italy the Allies continued to advance, and the Red Army had entered Yugoslavia. In the Pacific the Americans were preparing to retake the Philippines.

By October the British had been at war with Germany for more than five years, the Russians for more than three, and the Americans for nearly three. The strain on their armies was severe. It was a simple fact that the danger of being killed or maimed was causing psychological problems to many soldiers, who had now become veterans of the long campaign. The British commanders reckoned that after every twelve days of combat, a man should be given four days rest, estimating that he could remain unaffected by seeing the death of comrades, the constant fear of death or injury, for a period of 400 days combat before becoming likely psychiatric casualties. After five long gruelling years, that target was, on some occasions, just not realistic.

On 2 October Eugénie went into labour. For two whole days she lay soaked in sweat as the pain gripped her body. By 4 October she was growing weak and the Mother Superior called Albert to the chapel. 'We must pray, Monsieur, for your wife. I fear we have done all we can here. She needs to go to hospital and be treated by those who know more about childbirth than us.'

'I looked at her and knew what she was thinking. The only hospital in Alès was still run and staffed by the German military. I knew it was only a matter of days before they would have to leave, but that did not help me at that precise moment. It was bursting at the seams with their wounded, and

even if they were prepared to nurse Eugénie, the danger was that she could be recognised by the SS or the Gestapo. It was an agonising decision to make. I asked how long she would live if we chanced it and waited for the Allies to arrive, and the Mother Superior shook her head and said she could be dead within forty-eight hours. At least I knew then I had no alternative. I nodded and told the Mother Superior to do whatever she could.'

On 5 October Eugénie was admitted to the hospital as a nun, much to the amusement of the German doctors. *'How the Mother Superior must have hated that,'* wrote Albert, *'Her nuns were beyond reproach, and not one of them had fallen to the temptation of having an affair with one of the many SS officers who had constantly tried to make them break their vows. When I tried to thank the Mother Superior she just held up her hands and told me to pray for Eugénie and the baby.'*

On 9 October Eugénie gave birth to a boy. If it had not been for the German doctors she would certainly have died. On 11 October the Germans fled, and on the 16th an American doctor discharged her from the hospital.

'I often wonder what the Germans would have done to her if they had found out they were nursing the wife of someone they were longing to put up against a wall and shoot!' wrote Albert. *'I would love to think that our good fortune was a miracle brought about by the Mother Superior! Of course, it was no such thing, it was just her meticulous planning and another example of the Order's bravery. That they saved my life twice, and that of Annette's once, is beyond doubt. That they blackened the name of the Order in the eyes of God for Eugénie and my son, is still this very day something that brings tears of gratitude to my eyes.'*

They returned to the Convent for three more days before moving back to the Chateau. *'It was an emotional moment for us all, as we walked back through the front door,'* wrote Albert. *'Annette must have been thinking of Paul. Eugénie, I know, had been convinced she would never see the Chateau again, and I, with my boy held firmly in my arms, was longing to make contact with my family.'*

While Eugénie had been in hospital, Churchill had travelled to Moscow to talk to Stalin, not only about the final phases of the war, but also about their own countries' respective positions in a Europe free of the Nazi terror. Churchill was already beginning to worry about Stalin's claims to countries that the Red Army had liberated. They discussed Roumania, which Churchill acknowledged was 'very much a Russian affair'; Greece, which he felt was vital to Britain as a leading Mediterranean power, and

Poland. Churchill suggested that the German population of Silesia and East Prussia could be moved to central Germany. East Prussia could then be divided between Russia and post-war Poland, and Silesia given to Poland as compensation for the eastern area that Russia intended to annex.

Unknown to Albert, Mieszki Wielkie's fate was sealed at that Moscow meeting, and no Mieszkowski would ever again live in the house or oversee the land – the whole estate and all the possessions left in the house would eventually be confiscated by the Communist régime in Moscow. Albert's dream of one day inheriting the estate was blown away on the wind of change, and the cruel partition of so much of Eastern Europe.

On 12 April 1945, Roosevelt died at his home in Warm Springs, Georgia. The whole of the United States mourned, and battle-hardened soldiers wept. He was succeeded by his Vice-President, Harry Truman.

On the morning of 16 April the Red Army opened its offensive against Berlin with the firing of half a million shells, rockets and mortar bombs, and three thousand tanks drove westwards over the River Oder.

On 20 April, Hitler celebrated his fifty-sixth birthday, in a Berlin reverberating from the noise of Soviet guns, and on the 23rd, he assumed personal command of the defence of the city. The Hitler Youth, and men and women of all ages, were enlisted to try and keep the Russians from entering the capital.

On 28 April, in Italy, near the lakeside village of Dongo, Mussolini was shot dead by Italian partisans, and Hitler was contemplating the imminent destruction of his capital and his life's work.

In London, Churchill was growing ever more anguished at Stalin's behaviour over Poland. On 29 April, he telegraphed to the Russian leader: 'I have been much distressed at the misunderstanding that has grown up between us on the Yalta Agreement about Poland.' His concern was that Stalin had not allowed the Allies to select their 'democratic leaders' from the Free Polish in exile, or within Poland, to cooperate in the new Lublin government favoured by Stalin. This was in direct breach of the Yalta Agreement.

This bickering was briefly swept aside by the momentous news from Berlin, that at half past three in the afternoon of 30 April, Hitler had shot himself in the mouth. With this single shot, his dream of the Thousand Year Reich ended in ignominy. It had survived for twelve years – years of bloodshed, war, and indescribable evil.

On 8 May, British and American cities, bedecked with flags and banners, celebrated VE-Day, and throughout Western Europe there was excitement and relief that hostilities had ended. On 9 May in Moscow, Victory Day was welcomed by a salvo of a thousand guns, and Stalin proclaimed proudly on radio that, 'The age-long struggle of the Slav nations for their existence and independence has ended in victory. Your courage has defeated the Nazis. The war is over.'

PART THREE

MAY 1945 – AUGUST 1984

Chapter 13

Peace in Europe brought new worries for Albert. Emotions that he would much rather have ignored battered at his defences and threatened to overwhelm him once he had received information about the welfare of his family.

'Of course I had no idea if they had survived the war or where they were living, but I knew for certain that if they were alive, they would be worrying about me and I felt it my top priority to get a message to them. Communications in Alès were non-existent, and so I approached the Americans, who promised to do their utmost to help me. All I could do after that, was sit at the Chateau and wait. It was two long, agonising weeks before I received the news I had prayed for every night. My family had survived the war and were living in Scotland, and a message had been got to them to say that I was alive and well.

'Instead of making me feel more content, this news seemed to add to my restlessness and an unexplainable feeling of isolation. At first I couldn't understand why, but on reflection I realise it was three things. Firstly, I was suffering a form of withdrawal symptoms from all the danger I had experienced during the last five years. A common occurrence, I have now learnt, for those who were in continuous danger for so long. Secondly, at the back of my mind I was wondering if I had done the right thing by marrying Eugénie. That may sound cruel to any of my family who may one day read this diary, but the fact was, I had married her at a time of great stress without a great deal of thought for the future. Mainly, I think, because there seemed little future to look forward to. Now, that had all changed and, much as I hate to write it here, the truth was my love for her was not as deep as it should have been. I began to fear I had made a mistake. I felt, however, that I owed it to Annette to try and make a go of it,

and I kept telling myself that my love might grow, and that Eugénie's undoubted beauty might eventually sweep me off my feet. But as the weeks went by, my feeling of restlessness grew rather than waned, and I found it more and more difficult to hold Eugénie in my arms and actually say, "I love you." Nothing has changed since then.

Finally there was my country – Mieszki Wielkie, and the many friends I had left behind, not to mention my other concerns, like Jan Paderewski and Helene. I wondered endlessly about her, and was convinced that Jan had died in Budapest. My mind was in a turmoil. I felt alone in an unfamiliar environment that had seemed fine when we were at war, but which now lacked the ingredients which I needed to become once again a contented man. In truth, I missed my friends, family and country. I have been a difficult man to live with ever since.'

Poland in fact was on other people's minds as well – not least Churchill's. Once the euphoria of victory had died down, he had time to reflect again on Stalin reneguing on the Yalta Agreement. Alarm bells were ringing in London and Washington and Churchill conveyed his deep concern to Truman, ending by pointing out that the territories under Russian control, 'would include the Baltic provinces, a large slice of Germany, all Czechoslovakia, a large part of Austria, the whole of Yugoslavia, Hungary, Roumania and Bulgaria. It would include all the great capitals of middle Europe including Berlin, Vienna, Budapest, Belgrade, Bucharest and Sofia. This constitutes an event in the history of Europe to which there has been no parallel, and which has not been faced by the Allies in their long and hazardous struggle.'

In 1947, when Poland had finally become an integral part of the Soviet block, Albert wrote: *'Poor Poland no sooner had been liberated from the tyranny and evil of Nazism, than it was slowly but surely strangled by the strictures of Communist rule, and is now cut off from the freedoms that those in the West take so much for granted. The elections this year were a farce, and many people who opposed Communist rule were murdered, or driven out of the country, before a vote was cast. The Lublin men are in control, ruthless and subservient to the Kremlin. They broach no opposition, in case it threatens their idea of a perfect totalitarian State. None of the eastern block countries is allowed its own identity and, as far as I can gather, Poland is just another puppet of the Central Control. My poor country, my poor friends. At times I feel as if I'm a soul lost, locked forever out of my country. A man without a country is like a man without an identity, wandering aimlessly in a labyrinth of conflicting emotions.'*

The war in Europe might well have been over, but Japan remained un-bowed, although the tide was running strongly against her, and the Americans had chosen 1 November 1945 as the date for invading mainland Japan.

But on 16 July at half past five in the evening, the first atomic bomb was successfully tested at Alamogordo, New Mexico.

On 17 July, at the Potsdam conference, at which the Big Three were discussing the war with Japan, and the post-war settlement in Europe, Churchill was informed of the successful test, and on 22 July, he was given a detailed account of the effect of the atomic bomb on the test site. He immediately went into discussions with Truman. To the two men, the vision of finishing the war with one or two violent shocks, and so saving thousands of Allied lives, was irresistible.

On 24 July, Churchill, Truman and representatives from China sent a message to Japan offering her an opportunity to end the war. The demand was unconditional surrender of all Japanese Armed Forces. The message ended, 'The alternative is complete and utter destruction.'

Not waiting for Japan's reply, Truman told Stalin of the atomic bomb and then made plans to drop it no later than 10 August. He wrote in his diary, 'I gave instructions to use it so that military objectives and soldiers and sailors are the target, and not women and children. Even if the Japs were savages, ruthless, merciless and fanatic, we as the leaders of the world, for the common welfare, cannot drop this terrible bomb on the old capital or the new.'

He went on to confide in his diary. 'The target will be a purely military one and we will issue a warning statement asking the Japs to surrender and save lives. I'm sure they will not do that, but we will have given them the chance. It is certainly a good thing for the world that Hitler's crowd or Stalin's did not discover this atomic bomb. It seems to be the most terrible thing ever discovered, but it can be made the most useful.'

On 26 July the American cruiser *Indianapolis* arrived at Tinian Island with the atomic bomb. Waiting for it were the scientists who would assemble it and the air crew who would drop it. Even the aircraft that would carry the bomb had been chosen.

On 29 July, the *Indianapolis*, having left her deadly cargo, and on her way to Okinawa, was torpedoed just before midnight between Tinian Island and Guam. In the chaos that followed in the darkness more than 350 of her crew of 1,196 were killed in the explosion or went down with the ship. Another fifty died that night in the water. The following morning sharks attacked the survivors. There were no ships near to rescue the men and there had been no time for a distress call. Not until 2 August, when those that survived were spotted from the air, did anyone know the ship had even gone down. In all 833 men died in the disaster. For the Japanese it was a welcome success in an ever desperate situation.

On 30 July, Hiroshima was chosen as the target for the atomic bomb as, of the four target cities, it was the only one that did not have American prisoner-of-war camps.

On 2 August, American Intelligence learnt that Japan was still balking on unconditional surrender, in the hope that she could persuade Russia to mediate for her with the other Allies. With no sign of an unconditional surrender even being considered, the order was given to use the atomic bomb, and in the early hours of 6 August a B-29 bomber took off from Tinian Island with the bomb on board. Five and a half hours later Hiroshima caught the full horror of the first atomic bomb dropped on mankind, and 80,000 people were killed and 35,000 wounded. Of the 90,000 buildings in the city 62,000 were destroyed.

The Americans planned to drop another bomb on 11 August if, after Hiroshima, the Japanese did not surrender unconditionally, but because of predicted bad weather, this date was brought forward by two days. On the morning of 9 August, another atomic bomb was dropped on Nagasaki, exploding 1,650 feet above the city. This time 40,000 people were killed instantly, a further five thousand dying before the end of the year.

At midday on 15 August Japan surrendered unconditionally, and the Second World War was over.

A month later, when Albert learnt of the number of casualties suffered by the Japanese, he went for a long walk on his own. *'I felt sickened by this dreadful loss of life. I wondered then what the world had come to. Was bloodshed on this scale really necessary to solve man's arguments? How could any of us call ourselves civilised when we were prepared to spill so much blood? I sat down on the grass and looked up at the Chateau and made a decision. I would go to Paris and try to help some of the unfortunate Poles that had lost everything. Besides, I was tired of living in a vacuum – it was time to get back to the world I was used to. I would leave Eugénie and my son at the Chateau, until I had decided what to do. Was I running away from something I couldn't control, something that frightened me about my relationship with poor Eugénie? I know now I was.'*

Eugénie looked at Albert in amazement. 'Why Paris? If you want to leave here, take us back to England, where your family are. I understand that . . . but Paris? Do you not want me and your son?'

'*The truth was I didn't,*' wrote Albert, '*but how could I tell her that? I don't think she would ever have understood. So all I succeeded in doing was making a bloody mess of my reply, and making it quite obvious that I wanted to get away on my own. Her large blue eyes looked at me sadly. She didn't burst into tears or throw a temper. She just reached up and touched my face and said, "I will wait for you here, call for us when you are ready."*'

Albert left two days later, Annette refusing to say goodbye, and Eugénie looking at him in stunned amazement. Both women thought he was walking out on them for good.

On 30 September 1945 Albert arrived back in Paris, and made straight for the Polish Embassy in the Rue Tallyrand. He had no idea what he was likely to find. '*For all I knew, it was boarded up and empty, or full of a bunch of card-waving Communists. So my heart was in my mouth, as I walked down the street, wondering what to expect. I began to run – my breath coming in short gasps – the pain in my heart excruciating. And then I was at the door –the Polish flag was flying proudly above me! My God! I thought, I'm home! I stood by the door, looking at the brightly polished plaque. Would I be welcome, I wondered? There was only one way to find out! I stood still for a moment, controlling my breathing and regaining some of my composure, before reaching out to ring the bell!*'

Albert gazed in amazement at the two men standing opposite him. He had been convinced that both were dead. Yet here was Josef Milosz, a little more haggard, but still with his familiar heavy glasses perched precariously on his nose, and beside him, Jan Paderewski, slimmer and looking rather gaunt, but still with that twinkle in his eye.

'My God,' cried Albert as he embraced Jan and then shook Josef's hand. 'I never thought I would see you two again!'

Jan smiled. 'Nor I you!'

Josef shook his hand. 'Dear boy, I can't tell you how pleased I am to see you!'

An hour had passed since the Embassy door had swung open, and Albert had realised that at least nothing much had changed in the Rue Tallyrand. The furniture was all the same, the familiar curtains a little more faded, and even some of the domestic staff he recognised. When he had been taken to one of the Ambassador's aides and convinced him that he was indeed the Albert Mieszkowski that he had heard so much about from the Ambassador, he realised there was still a small part of Poland that had not yet been engulfed by the hammer and sickle.

'Sit down, sit down,' said Josef. 'I think we have a lot to tell each other. Would you like to begin, Albert?'

'*Once again I sat down in the familiar chair,*' wrote Albert. '*Nothing seemed to have changed since my last visit. I waited until the other two were settled before beginning my story. Only once was I interrupted, when a maid came in with some coffee.*'

'It seems to me you are lucky to be alive,' said Josef. 'Have you heard how your family are in England?'

'Yes, I managed to get the Americans to find out. They are well and living in Scotland. If I may, I will ring the Embassy in London today and obtain their number?'

'Of course, of course,' said Josef. 'Now, I think it is our turn, eh, Jan? You go first.'

Jan nodded and looked at Albert. 'I have been very lucky too. As you may know, the Embassy in Budapest was closed shortly after you left. Most of the staff managed to get to England but I decided to try and get back to Poland. It was a difficult decision, especially as I had hoped to marry Anna, but sometimes things just don't work out as you plan, do they? She had no need to flee Hungary – I did. So we parted. I think she would have come with me, but I couldn't allow her to put herself in so much danger. I have no idea what happened to her, and now I feel it is best if I don't try to find her. Once I got back into Poland I went to Warsaw and joined the AK – probably better known to you as the Home Army. We received our orders from London, and by 1944 were 400,000 strong. We had a very efficient network and derailed trains, blew up bridges, cut the German communications, and sabotaged military material like engines, equipment for tanks, guns and planes. Normally we did this sort of thing in the factories. Just after I arrived, we had to stop assassinations of German personnel as it provoked massive reprisals, but I can tell you we were still one hell of a nuisance to the Germans!

'One of our most spectacular attempts sadly went wrong. It was on 5 October 1939, when Hitler was taking the victory salute in Warsaw. Of course, I was in Budapest at the time, but people were still talking about it when I arrived in Warsaw. Not surprisingly when you think it might have changed the whole course of the war. The podium the bloody little man was going to stand on was packed with enough explosives to blow him and his entourage into the sky, but a last minute change of plan meant that our man responsible for detonating the charge was moved from the vicinity. Hitler never knew how lucky he was!

'Then finally, in August 1944, we took on the German army in Warsaw. Even without the help we had expected from the Allies we held out for sixty-three days before being defeated. No doubt you have already heard about that?'

'Yes, but I don't know any of the details.' said Albert.

'I will tell you another time, my friend, if you don't mind. This is a time to celebrate we are all alive. I don't want to feel anger today.'

Albert noticed Jan's hand was shaking. 'I understand – another day will do.'

Jan gave Albert a weak smile and continued. 'Well, I was one of the few lucky ones that escaped from that débâcle. Six of us broke away from a group of around five hundred hiding in a wood ten kilometres outside Warsaw, and made our way into the country. There we stayed until the Soviets drove the Germans out of Poland and in the chaos that followed we crossed into Hungary and eventually reached Trieste. I arrived here about ten days ago.'

'You seem to have been as lucky as me,' said Albert. 'By the law of averages I think we should both be dead! How about you, sir? Are you a lucky man too?'

Josef smiled at Albert. 'Inasmuch as I didn't have to put up with all the dangers you two young men faced, yes. In fact, listening to your stories makes me feel guilty at having spent the whole of the war in London. But I think I suffered in a different way. It was not easy, sitting inactive in London, with the German bombs falling around us, listening to the growing number of horror stories coming out of our country, and then, just as I began to think the worst was over, as the Germans were pushed back, I was forced to listen to how Stalin was tightening his grip throughout Poland. As you see, though, I have survived, a little older and even blinder, but I am lucky still to have a wife, my sanity and a job. I came back here six weeks ago as the Ambassador of the Government-in-exile, which, I hasten to add, is the only one I recognise – not those louts in Lublin, who are merely Stalin's lackeys. How long I will be here, is another matter. For soon I think it will be exile in England, as I can't see myself returning to my home in Poland. The death knell to democracy in our country, in my view, was sounded when the Allies recognised Stalin's compromise government, which included sixteen of his nominations out of a total number of twenty-one. Most of the ministers of the old Polish government are still in London, calling themselves the rightful Government of Poland. If only we could be left alone to sort out our own destiny. Since that is not to be, you mark my words, in a very short time Stalin will have full control over all of Poland. He already has stolen the east of Poland, and the Allies seem content to let him keep it.'

'I looked across at Josef's solemn face and knew he spoke the truth,'
wrote Albert. *'My dream of returning to Mieszki Wielkie crumbled at that
moment. As a member of a landowning family I would never be welcome
under a communist regime in Poland, let alone in the Soviet Union. I
realised that probably for the rest of my life I would be a refugee.'*

There was silence as Josef finished speaking, the two younger men busy
with their own thoughts. They had suffered a lot for the country they
loved, only for it to dawn on them that neither of them would return. *'In
spite of the joy at seeing each other, our celebrations were under a cloud
of uncertainty and some sadness,'* wrote Albert.

Josef coughed and stood up behind his desk. 'Enough of this depressing
talk. Let me get a bottle of champagne and we can enjoy being together
again.'

Once the bottle was on his desk, and their glasses had been filled, the
conversation almost inevitably turned to the suffering of the people of
Poland during the war. Albert, starved of true facts for so long, was
especially keen to hear from the other two how really bad it had been.
What he heard was an account of unbelievable barbarism, the full horror
of which took many months to be exposed.

The Nazis had started their extermination of the Polish population in
1939, murdering tens of thousands of Poles in the city of Bydgosxcz, 53
kilometres west of Warsaw. Political and cultural activities were forbidden; secondary schools, colleges and universities were closed down. As if
they needed to show their hatred of the educated classes completely the
Germans gathered 183 scholars in the Jagiellonian University of Kracow,
and deported them to the infamous concentration camp at Sachsenhausen,
where most of them died.

They ruthlessly exterminated eminent politicians and local dignitaries,
such as the heroic mayor of Warsaw, whose burial place is still unknown
today.

Nearly three million civilians were deported to Germany as slave la-
bourers and those left in Poland risked being stopped at random and shot
at public executions, or sent to concentration camps.

Numerous death camps were set up and, at Auschwitz alone, between
2.8 million (according to the Supreme National Tribunal in Poland) and 4
million (according to the Soviet State Commission for the investigation of
Nazi crimes at Auschwitz) perished in gas chambers, executions or as a
result of starvation, hard labour or disease. The Jewish ghettos were
slowly deprived of the means of livelihood, and thousands upon thousands of inmates died of starvation. However, the Germans decided that

the Jews were still not dying off quickly enough, so they proceeded to murder them outright, either on the spot or in special camps. At the beginning of the war there had been over three million Jews in Poland. Only a small number survived to see the Germans defeated, and they owed their lives to Poles who smuggled food to the ghettos, or who hid them at the risk of losing their own lives if discovered.

All methods of total extermination were used against Poles throughout the war, the Germans slaughtering defenceless people, and wiping out hundreds of villages all over the country, especially around Warsaw and the Zamosc region near Lublin. In all, over six million civilians lost their lives at the hands of the Nazis and amongst them were many friends of Albert's.

At four in the afternoon, a little the worse for wear from champagne, Albert made contact with his family. *'Without a doubt, it was the most emotional moment of my life so far. It is impossible to describe the wave of emotion that threatened to overwhelm me as I heard my father's voice, and then mother's, and finally Barbara's. I realised then how much I had missed them, how much I had relied on my father's good judgement, my mother's love and Barbara's sense of humour. It brought home to me even more vividly how wrong I had been to marry Eugénie. She could never fit into the pattern of our lives. Yet, as I told my father the news that I was married and had a son, his voice never once gave away whether he was disappointed or not. In fact he sounded genuinely pleased, and when he asked when I was coming to England with my bride and son, and I told him I was in Paris, and that she and John were in Alès, he mildly rebuked me for being a bad husband and father. At another time, I might have been irritated by his tone, but he could have said anything to me that day, so thrilled was I to be once again in contact with him. I think we talked for over half-an-hour, and by the time we had finished, I was determined to get to England as soon as I could.'*

Albert's chance came three months later. By that time he was beginning to think he should try to get Eugénie to join him in Paris, but when Josef asked him if he would like to join the Embassy in London, and help repatriate those Poles who wanted to return to Poland, he decided to leave her in Alès, and cross the Channel on his own. *'It was a strange decision, I know, but I told myself that I just wanted a little time on my own with my family, and to write up the diary. Both were pathetic excuses, but I couldn't quite bring myself to accept that our marriage was, to all intents and purposes, over. I wrote to Eugénie the day before I left, so that there was no danger of her contacting me before I reached England, telling her that once I had found a house I would bring her and John over. I promised her it wouldn't be long.'*

On 3 January 1946, Albert said goodbye to Josef and Jan. 'I think we have been here before,' laughed Josef. 'I hope this time it won't be so long before we meet again!'

Jan shook him firmly by the hand. He had plans to return to Poland and, in spite of both Josef and Albert trying to persuade him otherwise, he had not changed his mind. *'It was the last time I saw him,'* wrote Albert. *'What happened to him in Poland, I will never know. I had one letter from him two months after we parted, and then there was silence. I fear he must have been killed, no doubt still fighting for what he believed in, but against a different enemy. How many is it now? Andre Zaluski, Bartek Zablocki, Marek Radziwill, Lech Makowski, Gregori, Paul Jankowski, the Mother Superior and now Jan Paderewski. And Helene? Still no news – but still hoping! Oh God, will I ever be rid of the pain in my belly when I think of them?'*

London was grey and cold, and wrapped in the aftermath of the war. There was still rubble everywhere, and the people looked down-trodden and miserable. *'You would never have thought they had just won a great victory,'* wrote Albert, *'but then, what other country would throw their hero on the dust heap so soon after he had won the war for them!'*

The atmosphere in the London Embassy in Weymouth Street, was very different to the one in Paris. The celebration that Poland was free of the Nazis was dampened by the knowledge that she was now in the strangle-hold of Stalin's communist régime. Throughout the building there ran a deep feeling of resentment towards the British government for their re-fusal to recognise the government-in-exile down the road in Eaton Square, and for turning a blind eye to Stalin's blatant flouting of the Yalta agree-ment.

For two long months, Albert was confined to the Embassy, working with six other members of the staff desperately trying to deal with a regular flow of destitute Poles, who came to the Embassy door each day wanting to go home, find a job or try to trace relatives in Poland and in Europe. The forms piled higher every day on Albert's desk – the success rate was very low.

'I quickly discovered,' wrote Albert, *'that much to my surprise there were men and women who wanted to return to Poland. They were the relatively easy cases. The most difficult, and certainly the most distress-ing, were the ones trying to find relatives in a Europe which was on the*

*move with refugees, either fleeing from Communism, being forcibly re-
moved from their homes because of some border change, or desperately
trying to make their way home – if there was still one to go to! After all,
the whole area in the Ukraine, where Mieszki Wielkie was situated, was
now a no-go area for the Poles who had once lived there. There was, in
fact, a whole mass of people, like a million ants, crawling all over the
rubble of Europe, dazed and frightened. To find anyone in that chaos was
a miracle. More times than I like to keep count, we disappointed some
poor soul trying to find a relative; it was heartbreaking stuff, and I soon
plunged into a deep depression, which was made worse by the fact that I
had not yet been reunited with my family. Talking to them every day on the
telephone was simply not enough. The final blow to my sinking morale
came when at last I learnt of Helene's fate. As I cried over my desk that
morning, I decided for my own sanity I had to move. Anything would be
better than being cooped up in the distressing confines of the Embassy,
seeing every day the suffering caused to innocent people who were the
victims of a cruel war and an uncaring world.'*

His plea was listened to with sympathy, and nine weeks after arriving at
the Embassy, he was given a new posting in Spalding, Lincolnshire,
where many of the resettlement camps for Poles and other Europeans
were situated. But first he was allowed a week's leave to go and see his
family.

The Mieszkowskis had made several English friends over the years,
through the boar shooting at Mieszki Wielkie, and when they had arrived
in England in 1940, they had been offered hospitality by several of these
families. At first, Jacek and Krystina had chosen to remain in London,
while Barbara and Kasimir had gone to Scotland with the remnants of the
Polish army that had escaped to England. After six months in the capital,
Jacek decided it would be safer to move out, and took up the offer of a
cottage outside Keith in Aberdeenshire, on the estate of William Nickoll,
who had been a regular visitor for the boar shooting at Mieszki Wielkie
over several years.

On 10 March 1946, Albert was reunited with his family. *'I walked
through the door of the cottage on a freezing cold day and found mother
in the kitchen busy cooking something. I came to an abrupt halt, staring at
her for a few seconds in amazement and controlling with some difficulty
the urge to laugh. She used to tell me at Mieszki Wielkie that the only
things she would never do were housework or cooking, but the war had
obviously changed all that! She looked up startled, saw it was me, and
threw herself into my arms.*

'Once mother had stopped crying and dried her eyes, she dragged me through into a small, rather dark, sitting room where, huddled round a fire, were father and Barbara trying to keep warm from the Arctic wind blowing through the windows. I soon discovered that it blew almost unobstructed through the whole house, but nothing would have been able to dampen the joy I felt at once more seeing my family. It is difficult for me to put down on paper the emotions I felt, such was the excitement of actually being able to touch them, to see they were still flesh and blood. All I can write is that it was an amazing sensation that for several moments rendered me speechless. The next two hours are a time, even in my dotage, I hope I will always be able to remember.

'Father clasped me round the shoulders and I could see the dampness of his eyes. He looked thinner, and the lines on his face gave away that the five years since we had last seen each other had not been easy for him. Mother, gripping one of my hands as if she was frightened I would disappear again, was not dressed in her usual immaculate way, in fact looked quite untidy, and I even noticed stains on her blouse, something that she would never have tolerated at Mieszki Wielkie. Her clothes had always been spotlessly clean, her hair looking as if it had just been washed, and her fingernails beautifully manicured. It struck me that her new look rather suited her, although I'm quite sure she wouldn't have agreed.

'As for Barbara, she had changed the most, positively glowing with good health as she stood by the fire. I felt a little sad that the Dresden doll I had loved so much had gone, but was pleased to see the twinkle in her eyes, and the smile that stretched across her lovely face had not changed.

'There was so much to say to each other that we all started talking at once and for a while chaos reigned – but, oh God, what wonderful, wonderful chaos!

'Eventually, however, sanity returned and we settled down by the fire, drinking large cups of coffee served by mother – another first! – and listened to each others' stories.

'As soon as they had arrived in England, Kasimir had been sent to Scotland, where after a few weeks Barbara and their son André had joined them. There they had remained throughout the war, buying a house in Edinburgh in 1943, and when Kasimir had gone with the Polish 2nd Armoured Division to France, shortly after D-Day, Barbara had seen no reason to move. Besides, as she said, it was nice for her not to be too far from her parents, knowing what danger Kasimir was in. As I write he is still abroad and so I haven't yet met him, but hope to do so in the next week or so when he returns to England.

'My parents had remained in London during most of the blitz, Father recounting with some pleasure how, rather than go into shelter, he would venture out into Hyde Park at night during the air raids, and watch the anti-aircraft batteries pounding away at the enemy aircraft. Finally realising what a tremendous strain the bombing was putting on mother, he had agreed to move to the cottage. I got the impression that father had rather enjoyed London and was now bored, and missing his home and country, which was hardly surprising when I think what he was living in.

'It was inevitable that sooner or later questions would be asked as to why Eugénie was not with me, and I made all the excuses I could think of, but if I convinced mother, I knew I'd failed with father and Barbara, and when the two women eventually left the room to get some supper, father came straight to the point. Bluntly he told me that if I loved her, I should have her beside me. It was no way to treat a young wife with a son. He appreciated that I'd had a tough war, but really he felt that was no excuse.

'He was right of course. He nearly always was, and so I told him the truth, that the marriage was not all it should have been. I remember his reply so well, for it heralded the beginning of a new relationship between the two of us. To be honest I had expected more sympathy.

' "You have made your bed, boy. You come from a family of honour, and of strict Catholic upbringing, and I expect you to act like a true Polish gentleman. Go back to France and bring the poor girl here and make an effort to put a life together, if only for the sake of your son. Sacrifices have to be made in life."

'Sacrifices! My God, have I not sacrificed enough already? My blood boiled, and I had great difficulty in not shouting at him. I had to swallow bloody hard before retorting that it was all right for him to lecture me when he'd had such a happy marriage, but he could have no idea how I was suffering. His reaction was probably typical of someone who thought he was the only loser in the war. He ignored what the war had done to other people, uprooting them from homes which they would never see again, causing untold hardship, fear and remorse. There is no doubt in my mind that the reservoir of human pain built up in the war years had a long time yet to run, but he didn't understand all that, why should he have done? He had led a life of pampered luxury up until the war – cocooned against the vagaries of life. He had been brought up in a privileged society, mixed with the privileged few, and never once had to fend for himself. He had no idea what I had gone through in the war, could never begin to understand the pain I felt at losing so many friends, and could *never know what it was like to live every second in fear for one's life. Before I completely lost control of myself I escaped to the women in the kitchen. Later, as I lay alone in bed on my first night at the cottage, thinking of Helene rather than Eugénie, I realised that the passage of time had forced father and me a little apart. Our views on life were so different.*

'Now, a week later – I leave for Spalding in the morning – during which time Barbara has taken me to see André and handed over my diary, I know that what I was thinking that night is the truth. The ease with which father and I used to converse has gone; there is a tension between us, and I know some of the reason is Eugénie, the other is my more liberal views, which he heartily disapproves of. I suppose it is understandable – he is living in what he sees as an alien world and misses Mieszki Wielkie and Poland. My God, so do I, but the difference is that I saw disaster coming and have been forced to adapt to the changed situation. He hasn't, and never will. He is happy to ignore the present and live in the past. Tomorrow I will be quite relieved to go. I just pray that father and mother don't realise this. As for Barbara, I know she thinks like me, but feels I'm being too impatient with him, and hard on Eugénie. But who is she to lecture me? She has a home, a child and a husband she loves.

'The words I have just written leave me to feel that I'm a little bitter. It surprises me, for I didn't think I was that sort of person. Now maybe I am. Having re-read the sentences again there are definite signs. I must not let bitterness enter my life. It can eat one away so easily. I must strive to remain understanding, and to remember that I'm one of the lucky ones to have survived. I must never, never forget that, or all my friends' deaths will have been in vain.'

Chapter 14

The Nissan hut that was allocated to Albert, at the Displaced Persons camp near Spalding, did not suit him at all, and within a week he had rented a small house on the outskirts of the town and bought a bicycle, and at eight o'clock every week-day morning, he set out for the camp.

The camp was full of many Europeans, casualties of the aftermath of war and changing borders. Albert's task, as at the London Embassy, was mainly to help the Poles who wanted to return to Poland. At first, many of these were from the landowning classes, filled with a misplaced fervour to help their country. Although they had many reservations about the Soviet Union, they felt nothing could be worse than the Nazis. Not many months were to pass by, however, before some were to return to Britain, disillusioned by the ever-increasing lack of freedom and the heartbreaking sight of their estates confiscated and split up amongst the peasants.

A large majority who found themselves stranded in England chose not to return to Poland and, however great the hardships, the wisdom of their choice quickly became apparent. Fear was going to be the method by which those in power were to rule Poland, and soon the security service, known as the UB, were haunting every aspect of society. There was not a single person that did not qualify for their attention. Poland had got rid of the Gestapo, only to find itself wrapped in the tentacles of an organisation just as menacing.

Once more, Albert found himself deeply depressed. Post-war England was not the easiest place to find a job, and the majority of the people he was trying to re-settle were army personnel or from the professional classes, such as doctors, dentists, lawyers and school teachers, who did not have their qualifications recognised by the British government. Soon London's smart hotels, like the Savoy and the Dorchester, had Polish colonels and lawyers washing up dishes in their kitchens or taking menial jobs in factories. Nothing was refused, and at one time, almost the entire staff at the J Lyons bakery near Olympia consisted of officers from the Polish 2nd Armoured Division. England, though, was not the only country open to them, and many sailed to Australia, America and South Africa, and a few to Canada and Argentina, to start a new life.

Of course, not all the refugees were in England, and from the liberated concentration camps and Displaced Persons Camps in central Europe, a vast tide of people was on the move, not least the Jews. Some were returning to devastated towns, or going to England or the United States, but by far the most popular destination was Palestine. Although the British Government tried desperately to limit the number of immigrants, thousands managed to make their way to Palestine illegally.

By the beginning of 1947, Barbara was expecting her second child, and Albert was travelling to another camp near Kirkham, in Lancashire, dividing his time as best he could between the two camps. It was exhausting work both physically and mentally and he was ready for some much deserved leave.

Apart from the odd weekend spent with his parents or Barbara, he had been working almost non-stop for ten months. He was denied the peace that he so desperately sought during the weekends at Keith, as his father continuously pressed him to bring Eugénie and his son over to England. 'Your mother and I wish to see our grandson,' he would say, time and time again, glaring at Albert, who would bite out a bad-tempered reply, which would lead to his father not speaking to him for the rest of the weekend. It was painful for them to see their relationship deteriorating in front of their eyes, but both of them were too proud to admit that either of them was at fault.

So he relied on his weekends with Barbara for peace and quiet, and it was while playing with his young nephew that he realised he missed his son, and that he would have to return to France. Besides, the pressure from his family was building up such a head of steam that he feared his father might never speak to him again unless he visited Alès. So, when he was given three weeks leave in March, he braced himself to return to the Chateau. *'I would rather not be going,'* he wrote the night before he left England, *'But quite honestly, I can't take father's disapproval and mother's hang-dog looks any longer. Besides, it will be nice to see John.'*

His stay at the Chateau was not a success. Annette castigated him even more than his father, and Eugénie's looks said it all. He was delighted, however, to be reunited with his son. *'I was thrilled to see the boy, and because of this, I put up with Annette's constant flow of anger and Eugénie's disapproving silences. We slept in the same bed, and every now and then as she lay in my arms, I felt the old desire. The nights, in fact, were the best –no Annette to encourage her daughter – just the dark room and a woman in my arms who could been anyone.'*

He stayed for two weeks. By then he had vowed never to return to Alès. He found Annette intolerable. *'Understandable, I suppose, given that she was convinced I was about to desert them both. Sadly, our friendship had deteriorated. As well as this, the town held too many memories of Gregori and Paul for me to feel at ease.'*

On his last night he promised Eugénie that he would send for her as soon as his work was completed at the camps and he could settle down in one spot for more than a fleeting moment. By the looks he received as he left, he knew that the two women did not believe him.

Albert did mean what he said, for he felt it was time he had his son around him. *'In the few brief moments that I was able to spend with him alone, I realised how much he meant to me, and one day I'm determined to get him away from the Chateau and Annette's influence.'*

His work kept him too busy to do anything about it until February 1948. That month Barbara gave birth to a daughter, who was christened Krystina Jane, and when Britain recognised the Polish government, the Communists sent their new Ambassador to London. The camp in Lancashire closed, and it would only be a few months before Spalding said goodbye to its last inhabitants. It was almost time for Albert to look for alternative employment, and for that he needed his wits about him and someone to give him two square meals a day. So he wrote to Eugénie asking her to come to England with their son. He was not at all sure she would leave her mother but, unknown to him, Eugénie had fallen for a young Englishman visiting Alès in the autumn of 1947, and so his letter gave her the opportunity she was looking for.

She arrived in Scotland in March 1948. By that time, with financial help from his father, Albert had bought a house close to Barbara in Edinburgh, having convinced him that he had every intention of bringing Eugénie over as soon as he could, and was well on his way to finding a new job. Opportunities were limited, but he soon discovered that being a Polish aristocrat, doors were opened that might well have stayed closed. It was not long before he was under pressure to enter the field of finance.

'Nothing impresses the English more,' he wrote, *'than a well bred Pole, turned out in a smart suit, with a striped shirt, a silk tie and well polished shoes. The fact that I have little money, and even less experience, is of no*

consequence, and I'm assured that I will have no difficulty picking up a job once my duties in Spalding are finished.

'*The weekends in Scotland are becoming quite hectic, with lunch and dinner invitations landing on my desk with encouraging frequency. I can't deny I'm flattered. An enjoyable bonus is the attractive women I meet at these parties, some of whom quickly look upon me as a possible catch. It quite hurts to have to tell them I'm already married!*'

The arrival of Eugénie, however, put an end to this socialising, and after a week staying with his parents, during which time he watched with some satisfaction his father's growing disapproval of her, they moved to the house in Edinburgh. '*I can't help thinking that father now wishes I had left her in France!*' he wrote. '*Of course, he does his best to hide his feelings from me, but mother is not so reticent, sighing loudly every time she speaks to me about Eugénie – an old trick she used with us during our childhood to show her disapproval. At least they are thrilled with their grandson, and of course father is much too much of a gentleman to do anything but make Eugénie feel welcome. One encouraging outcome of all this, is that my bitterness has faded away, and although father and I will never be as close, at least we respect each other again. It sounds callous, but I'm delighted that my parents do not approve of Eugénie, for I'm finding each day with her more difficult. I'm fortunate in that I still have to go to Spalding during the week, and so get away from her for a considerable time. I never offer to take her with me.*'

Then out of the blue in July, Eugénie announced that she was pregnant. '*No one is more surprised than me!*' Albert wrote. '*I looked at her in amazement when she told me this morning and I feel my reaction upset her. I hesitate to write too much here, as my suspicions could well be unfair. I'm trying to work out how many times we have shared a bed in the last few months. Luckily, perhaps, my memory is hazy. That way at least there is a chance the child is mine.*'

From then on the tension between the two of them increased and he treated her with great suspicion. '*I have become rather furtive, sneaking looks at her letters as they come through the post box and wondering where she is when I'm away in Spalding. I don't want to find out anything, but man grows naturally inquisitive when he thinks a wife is straying.*'

Never once did he voice his doubts to anyone and when, in February 1949, Eugénie gave birth to a little girl, he appeared as pleased as any one else, but the birth did nothing to improve the marriage, and by now the couple were thoroughly unhappy in each other's company. Albert knew it could only be a matter of time before one of them broke, and he was not surprised when it was Eugénie who made the move, leaving their son John with him, and taking their daughter Ewa to live with another man.

'It had to happen,' Albert wrote the day after she had left. *'It hurts me to think that we had grown so far apart, and that a love that had seemed unbreakable at the time of our marriage has turned so sour, but she prefers another man to me, and I can't say I have done much to change her mind since she came over from France. Now at last the charade is over, and I must be thankful for her leaving me John. I'm surprised, but grateful that she didn't want to hurt me too much. I presume that soon she will come crying for a divorce – of course I cannot give her one. My Catholic faith, and Father's wrath prevents me.'*

Albert's parents were very keen for him and his son to join them in Keith, but he was determined to keep his independence and insisted on remaining in Edinburgh. With Barbara so close, there was no problem with John, and even when Kasimir returned from France, Barbara continued to look after the boy when Albert was away.

For the first time since he had met Helene, Albert felt more at ease with himself, and in February 1950, when his job at Spalding, finally and rather belatedly, came to an end he took up the offer of employment as an underwriter in London, keeping his house in Edinburgh and once again with his father's help buying one in Chelsea. For the first five months he returned to Scotland every weekend to be with John, but once he found himself on a sound financial footing and could exist without handouts from his father, he employed a nanny in London, and took John with him to the capital.

His parents thoroughly disapproved of this move, voicing their opinion that Scotland was a far healthier place to bring up a young boy than smog-ridden London, but Albert was in no mood to listen, determined to put the last few years behind him and start to enjoy all the things he had missed. *'I was determined to enjoy myself before another war befell us. I had wasted too many years already – I wanted some fun, some good women, and some money.'*

He was soon in much demand at parties, working hard during the day, and dancing or dining most evenings, but he still resolutely turned down any weekend invitations, always content to return to Scotland so that his family could see John.

As he feared, Eugénie became a thorn in his side. A month after walking out, she began what turned into a weekly bombardment of demands for a divorce. Soon he was sick to death of her pestering him. *'But I won't give in to her! Why the hell should I?'*

Eventually, in October 1950, Eugénie gave up trying and changed her name by deed poll. The day she told him he wrote, '*Thank God for that, now maybe I will get some peace. In many ways, I'm glad she no longer bears my name. I keep asking myself if I would have married her in different circumstances and the answer is always "no". So I have only myself to blame. It was a time of madness, when one did things as if there would be no tomorrow. If I had died my family, would have been delighted that I had married her and produced an heir, and she would have mourned for me. The mistake was we both survived the war! God, that sounds cynical, but it is the truth nevertheless.*'

On 6 May 1951 Jacek Mieszkowski celebrated his seventieth birthday, and held a family party at the cottage in Keith, which he had bought eighteen months before. All the family were present except for John's sister Ewa, who had never been allowed to visit her grandparents, and whom Albert had seen only once since she had been born. '*I have almost forgotten I have a daughter,*' he wrote, '*And to be honest, I would now rather not see her, for what is the point of upsetting myself and her if I'm never going to be allowed to be her father. Perhaps I'm not anyway, but young John makes up for what I'm missing. He is growing into a fine lad, and I think will be a true Mieszkowski.*'

The party was tinged with a little sadness, because it had always been Jacek's wish to return to Poland before he was seventy and, as he cut his cake, on top of which Barbara had made an exact replica in marzipan of Mieszki Wielkie, his eyes filled with tears. 'It is wonderful to have all my family around me today, and thank you for the presents. It is only sad that we are not gathered round the dining room table at Mieszki Wielkie for this moment. My father and grandfather celebrated their seventieth birthdays there and it has always been my wish ever since we fled to do the same.' He turned to Albert. 'I can now only pray that you or your son will be able to follow in their footsteps.'

Albert knew the chances of either of them doing that were very remote. The steel hand of Stalin had a firmer grip than ever on Eastern Europe, and now that Mieszki Wielkie was part of the Ukraine, any last hope of a Mieszkowski going back to the house had disappeared in the wind. Nevertheless, he raised his glass to his father and said, 'If the chance comes we will return, and besides, who knows, you might be back there for your eightieth!'

That evening, in the quietness of his room, he wrote, '*Everyone knew there wasn't a hope, even father, but no one said a thing, and those that*

*remembered it drank to his beloved Mieszki Wielkie, and his two grand-
sons rushed over and kissed him.'*

The very nature of the Poles always held out the tantalising possibility to
those such as Albert and his family, that one day they might be able to return,
not to Mieszki Wielkie, but at least to a free Poland with its new frontiers,
for throughout all Polish society democracy, legality and God were wor-
shipped. This was an anomaly in a Marxist state, and it baffled and annoyed
those that had embraced and now enjoyed the privileges of communism.
This deep and enduring faith was backed by the Church, at first allowed a
certain amount of freedom, mainly because the authorities found it difficult
to persecute an institution that had taken an uncompromising stand against
the Germans at great cost to its priests. By 1949, however, it had become too
much of a threat to the authorities, and all its lands were nationalised. At the
same time all religious instruction was forbidden in schools, and in 1952
three bishops and several priests were put on trial charged with spying for
the United States. The Party however were always nervous of acting too
harshly towards an institution that had enormous peasant support, and could
still prove to be the rallying point for democracy in spite of the persecutions.
When, twenty-one months after Jacek's seventieth birthday, on 3 March
1953, Stalin died, many Poles within and outside the country felt that this
could herald a new move, however slow, towards eventual democracy.

During that time, Albert's financial position continued to improve, and
he repaid much of the money he owed his father. *'He objects, of course,
but my pride is at stake and I think he understands that.'*

By now he had become integrated into the London Polish 'set', and was
a well known figure at all the best parties. Women flocked round him, and
he was not slow to show them his affection. *'I have lost count of the
number who wish to become my mistress, and some even aspire to marriage, but I'm not ready for that yet – none of them could hold a candle to
Helene for beauty or intellect. To be honest, I find behind most of their
beauty an amazing lack of knowledge, or interest in anything else but
flirting! As long as I keep it this way it is fun, and most rewarding! The
men, however, are far better informed, and sometimes I like to go to my
club and talk about Poland, because however much I'm enjoying myself,
I'm well aware of being a man with no home.'*

In fact, as the Poles had hoped, Stalin's death did ease the iron grip
from Moscow, and that flicker of light began to burn a little stronger.
Even Albert, as pessimistic about Poland's future as anyone in London,
began to see a new era for his poor oppressed country.

The 'Thaw' emanating from the Kremlin didn't amount to much, but at least the paranoia of the last few years receded, although no one could yet call themselves free from the prying eyes of the State. However, writers who had not dared put their doubts about the party system on paper for years, now appeared in print questioning, albeit in veiled terms, the principles of communism, and whether all the Marxist-Leninist economic theories were as foolproof as the party would like everyone to believe.

Then, early in 1954, a Colonel Jozef Swiatlo, who was deputy chief of the Tenth Department, defected to the West, and broadcast on Radio Free Europe the inside story of the hated UB. To the astonishment of the people and even of some senior Party members, they learnt exactly how much every aspect of their lives had been dictated by Moscow. It created quite a furore; the Party quietly released many political prisoners from prison, the Head of the UB was dismissed, and the security service thought it wise to take a lower profile. The Party began to admit they had made mistakes – a dangerous move when it had no idea how Moscow would react, and so the Polish Party secretary, Bierut, played a canny game, dithering between thaw and repression. He was inclined to favour the latter, as were many traditionalists in the Party, and the people were left to hope and wonder.

In February 1956, Khrushchev denounced Stalin's rule, and Bierut, appalled by such treachery, immediately died of a heart attack and the Party was thrown into disarray. Khrushchev came to Warsaw to attend the plenary session of the Party's Central Committee, which would choose a new Party secretary, and Edward Ochab, regarded as a liberal amongst the traditionalists, was elected and immediately began a programme of liberalisation, a partial amnesty, which led to the release of nearly 70,000 political prisoners, and the arrests of several high-ranking officers of the UB.

By October the reforms had led to unrest, which culminated in workers in Poznan attacking a police station, and the headquarters of the UB. When they went on to demolish the town's radio jamming station, the authorities called in the tanks and the riots ended in bloodshed.

This gave the Stalinist die-hards the opportunity to call upon Moscow for help, and Khrushchev obliged, by arriving in Warsaw on 19 October, having secretly ordered Soviet troops to march on Warsaw. Bloodshed was averted by Wladyslaw Gomulka, who managed to convince Khrushchev that he could contain the situation, and the troops were ordered back to their barracks. When Gomulka spoke to a huge rally in Warsaw on the 24th, he promised socialism with a human face and a

Polish tinge. As a first move Cardinal Wyszyhaski was released from prison, and the Church was allowed to resume its normal activities, providing it pledged its allegiance to the new régime. Hundreds of Soviet officers were dismissed from the Polish army, and a quarter of a million Poles trapped inside the Soviet Union were allowed to emigrate to Poland.

As Albert and his friends feared, however, the changes were largely cosmetic. They were convinced that nothing much had really altered, and that if the State was ever challenged it, would not take long for the Soviet troops to be back in Warsaw. When, on 30 October, Imre Nagy declared a return of democracy to Hungary, their fears were rapidly proved correct as, five days after his announcement, thousands of Soviet troops and hundreds of tanks invaded Hungary.

'*It is as I feared,*' wrote Albert on 6 November, '*Communism will not die that easily in Poland. It might like to show a softer face to the western world, but deep down it is as repressive as ever, especially when it sees itself threatened, as it is in Hungary. In my view, it will be a long time before any of us here in England can once again walk around the streets of Warsaw as citizens of a democratic Poland.*'

A few stumbling steps however had been taken in the right direction, and in his club Albert could sense the new air of optimism that prevailed amongst its Polish members, but he was sure they were catching at straws, and wrote, '*I feel, however, that many of those thinking about packing their suitcases will have a very long wait, and some will almost certainly be dead by the time communism in Poland is defeated. In fact, when asked if I ever see this as a possibility, my answer is in the negative.*'

In England, most people would have agreed with him, for Gomulka's tenancy at the head of the Polish government was never secure, and even though a purge of Stalinists was carried out in the ranks of the Party, he still had many enemies left just waiting for the chance to strike at his more liberal way of government.

When, much to the Polish government's embarrassment, the open collecting of funds and medical supplies for the Hungarian freedom-fighters forced it to vote against the Soviet Union at the United Nations, the days of Gomulka's liberalism were numbered, and by 1959 the democratic façade of the Party was exposed as a myth. Albert's pessimism had been well founded.

Chapter 15

By 1959, Albert was a well established Lloyds underwriter, and with John now boarding at Sherborne, he was freer than ever to indulge his taste for young decorative women. His father was continually urging him to get married. 'I want to see a beautiful girl on your arm before I die,' he said almost every time he saw Albert. *'But I'm having a ball,'* Albert wrote, *'Why on earth should I marry and make another mistake? There is safety in numbers! I think father may well be disappointed.'*

There was, however, one of his father's disappointments that Albert had been striving to make sure he could remedy. He had never given up hope of taking him back to Poland before he died, and once the so-called thaw came, he continually badgered the Polish Embassy in London for visas. His hopes were fairly high until once more the pendulum swung the wrong way. *'I didn't stop trying, only because I knew it gave father something to live for.'* And no sooner had he decided his chances had dropped to zero, than he was invited to call at the Embassy. It was the most positive move yet.

The night before his appointment, he quelled the urge to ring his father and spent a sleepless night wondering if at last the authorities had relented. *'I sat up drinking coffee and praying for father to get his wish, and when dawn came I bathed and shaved, and was at the door of the Embassy half-an-hour before it opened.'*

Alas, he was to be bitterly disappointed, for although for some weeks the Embassy kept making the right noises, the stamp on the passport never came, and finally, on 5 January 1960, his application was turned down. *'I can only bless the moment I decided not to say a word to father. It is bad enough for me, but for him – well, I think it might have killed him.'*

In spite of his father's continuous questions about the visas, Albert never told him that they had been refused. *'In fact, I tell him that I'm still trying, although I don't think he believes there is a chance in hell, and I can see that the light has gone from his eyes. Mother says he is sleeping badly and harps back to their life at Mieszki Wielkie more and more. Poor father, I'm afraid he may die of a broken heart.'*

In fact two months after writing this, his father was dead, having contracted pneumonia after falling down the stairs of the cottage and breaking a leg. *'I think at the end he was relieved to die,'* wrote Albert. *'It is the end of a grand old man, and I will miss him terribly. Oh yes, we had our disagreements, and inevitably we grew a little apart, but I have never lost my respect or my love for him. I know he suffered terribly in his latter years from being robbed of Mieszki Wielkie, but he never once allowed his deep distress to affect his love for us all. I will mourn him for many months.'*

Two months later Barbara persuaded her mother to sell the house at Keith and go and live with her. Albert wrote. *'Kasimir is mumbling a bit, but I'm sure he will get over it. Besides I couldn't possibly have her here – I don't think she would approve of my way of life!'*

The women in his life, and there were many at that time, had to play second fiddle to John during the school holidays, for Albert spent every free moment with his son. In the winter and spring this was normally in London. In the summer they always stayed with Barbara and Kasimir. It was a time when Albert thought Scotland was at its best, and it was here that he got closest to his son. *'I taught him to fish and would spend hours in the garden of the house talking to him about Poland and Mieszki Wielkie. Now father is dead, I'm more than ever determined to go back to my country one day. Mieszki Wielkie, alas, is now only a fool's dream.'*

The '60s for Albert were full of excitement and increasing financial independence. His business acumen was paying handsome dividends, his relationship with John grew in strength, and much to his surprise he fell in love. Although still uneasy about some aspects of his life, such as never making any attempt to see his daughter Ewa, or to take John to see Eugénie, it was a time when he found that at last he was at peace with himself, and capable of coping with the memories of the war, which had for so many years been troubling him. *'I will never forget my dead comrades,'* he wrote, *'However, at least now I find I can push them to the back of my mind with a little less guilt.'*

The reason for his more relaxed state of mind was undoubtedly his love for Alicia Pachalska, a thirty-four-year old Pole, who at the age of eighteen had fought alongside her redoubtable mother Catherine in the Warsaw uprising. Catherine had been quite a character in Warsaw before the war, well known as a leading light of the 'café society'. She had also had extremely bad luck with her husbands. Her first one was lost in an accident on an army firing range outside Kracow, but not before he had fathered her only child. Her second husband had been killed with the Polish army in May 1944, during the final assault on Hill 593 at Monte Cassino. Today there is a cemetery on the hill with a massive stone Virtuti Militari Cross at the entrance. An inscription reads; 'Go tell the Poles, thou that passest by, that here obedient to their laws we lie.'

Her third husband, Rudolf Soltysik, she married in Italy after the war. She had chosen Italy as soon as she and Alicia had been freed from a munitions factory in the Ruhr where they had both been deported by the Germans after the Warsaw uprising collapsed.

Soltysik, who had been a gynaecologist before the war in Warsaw when he had known Catherine briefly, had gone with General Anders and his army to Russia after the fall of Poland, and when hostilities ceased in 1945, he had made his way to Italy via Turkey and Greece. Neither he or Catherine had wanted to stay in Italy and so in 1948, a year after marrying, they had moved to England. Sadly, once again she was to lose a husband prematurely, and in 1960 he died of a heart attack.

Alicia had inherited her mother's rather wild gypsy looks and enormous sense of fun and Albert found her irresistible. *'She is clever, witty and beautiful in a wild uncontrolled way and, like Helene, very sensuous. Her mother is another plus, being one of the funniest women I have ever met, and full of the joys of life, in spite of losing three husbands and working the last year of the war as a slave for the Germans. They are incorrigible and I'm smitten by them both.'*

In early 1961, he contacted Eugénie and, forgetting his Catholic upbringing, offered her a divorce, which she accepted with alacrity, and on 10 September he and Alicia were married, but not before he had made sure John was happy with the proposed union. *'I'm not quite sure what I would have done if he had run out of the room saying he hated her! Thank God, he seemed to approve, and I feel they will get on well together.'*

They settled in London, but kept the house in Edinburgh, although Alicia was not as fond of Scotland as Albert. London and Albert had captured her heart, and they were soon entertaining various different echelons of London society, but enjoying most the evenings with Catherine and her gypsy friends, some of whom were Poles, and others Hungarians who had fled their country in 1956. The singing and dancing went on long into the night and Albert wrote: *'These are the happiest times I have had since leaving Poland. These people are so different, so*

*relaxed and friendly, and all of us bound together by a common bond –
refugees from our countries. This seems to draw us even closer together.'*

Albert's mother was not sure how to treat her new daughter-in-law.
Alicia was definitely not the sort of woman that she had envisaged her son
marrying, after the disaster with Eugénie, but in a short while she grew
quite fond of her, and was always insisting that whenever they came to
Scotland they visited her. 'I'm growing older,' she said to Albert, 'And I
want to see as much of you and John as I possibly can.' She never
mentioned Albert's daughter.

Albert settled easily into married life. '*Slightly surprised,'* he wrote the
morning after he and Alicia had celebrated their first anniversary. *'I felt at
first that again I might have gone into this one in too much of a rush, but
I'm now confident that my worst fears were groundless. Alicia has
brought home to me just exactly what a happy union can do to a man. I
now understand how father must have felt. I'm indeed a man with no
conflicts of conscience.'*

On the other hand, the '60s for Poland threw up conflicting signals. A
General Mieczyslaw Moczar had been placed in charge of the secret
service to tighten up security, and a new campaign of petty persecution
was launched against the Church. This time, the Party stood back from
repression and replaced it with obstructionism and judicial harassment. In
spite of this, the Church went from strength to strength, the drabness of
everyday socialist life comparing badly with the beauty of the Catholic
faith. The priest was the one person to whom society could always turn.
The younger generation, who had not known the deprivations of the war,
grew more and more disillusioned with communism in whatever form.
Gomulka's reign was drawing slowly to a close, and although he had been
forced to revert to the old-fashioned methods of reactionary communism,
the likes of General Moczar saw him as soft and incompetent, and were
just waiting for their chance to overthrow him. The new generation's
dream of democracy was still a long way off.

General Moczar's chance came in 1967, with the Six-Day War between
Israel and the Arabs. The Soviet Union and her satellites were on the side
of the Arabs, but the Israeli victory was greeted with delight in Poland,
partly because it was a chance to deal a slap in the face to Russian policy,
and partly because Polish society could identify with the Jews, since
many of whom were of Jewish origin. People could hardly hide their
delight that the Arabs had been defeated.

In January 1968, General Moczar saw this as a chance to attack the
students and brand them as 'Zionist'. Gomulka made an inept speech that

all Jews were not 'Zionists', but fingers were already being pointed at the Jewish origins of the student leaders, and even at some high ranking members of the Party. Soon a number of senior officials were being dismissed, and student unrest was savagely dealt with.

Gomulka, whose own wife was Jewish, hung on to power with grim determination, well aware that the witch-hunt was deflecting much of the criticism of his own leadership. His position however was tenuous and he had to rely on Soviet support, buying it with participation, in August, in the invasion of Czecholslovakia. This did nothing to strengthen his popularity amongst the people or the Party, for included with all his other troubles was the economy, which was rapidly disintegrating. Wages slumped, working conditions declined, and the private sector in agriculture was starved of investment. Socialist principles demanded that it should eventually be phased out, but in Poland private enterprise was responsible for 80% of all production. The confusions were catastrophic and, following two bad harvests in 1969 and 1970, the country was ready to explode.

On 13 December 1970 basic food prices were raised by 30%. The reaction to this was immediate, with workers at the Lenin Shipyard in Gdansk going on strike and marching in protest to the local Party headquarters. The police guarding it opened fire on them, but were soon overwhelmed and the building burnt down. Similar strikes and confrontations took place in nearby Gdynia and Szczecin. The Party could not allow such behaviour to go unchallenged, and the next day ordered the tanks to move in. The fighting spread to other cities on the coast and on 17 December, the whole area was sealed off by the army. The fighting was hard and one-sided, and hundreds of workers were killed.

On the 19th, the Politburo voted to replace a sick Gomulka with Edward Gierek, who managed to woo the workers with his apparent goodwill, but it was not until the price rises were rescinded that the strikes ended.

Gierek commented, 'The episode is a painful reminder that the Party must never lose touch with the working class and the nation.' Many people believed him, but the next ten years were to show that, although he looked upon himself as a 'modern Communist', and his new détente with the West meant that foreign capital flowed into his country, and the economy improved, he had learnt nothing from the traditional, unimaginative, and committed communists of the Gomulka era. Very slowly, an unbridgeable chasm grew between him and the people of Poland.

To Albert, like those in Poland, Gierek seemed to be the new face of a softer and more understanding Party and he hoped that this might work to his advantage with regard to a visa. Once more he started writing to the Embassy and once more a visa was refused. He was bitterly disappointed, and on one of his visits to his mother he confessed that he feared he might never get his wish.

It was on one of these visits in February 1972 that his mother fell ill and two weeks later died. *'She will be happy in death,'* wrote Albert. *'She will meet father again, tell him that I'm content at last with an extraordinary woman, whom she can't quite understand, and talk to him about the wonderful years at Mieszki Wielkie.'*

From then on Albert's visits to Scotland became less regular. John was now working, and Alicia hated the winters, preferring to stay in the warmth of their home in Chelsea. They never went abroad for a winter holiday. *'The day I cross the Channel again will be to go to Poland,'* wrote Albert. But he refused to sell the house in Edinburgh, and in the summer still managed to drag Alicia across the border to spend a little time with Barbara or alone in their house. *'I love it in Edinburgh, it is the only time I have alone with Alicia. No parties, just peace and the warmth of her presence.'*

He settled down to a period that he later wrote had been the happiest of his life, and his joy was made complete when, on 6 April 1974, John married Vicky Davies, at Narberth village church, in the county of Pembrokeshire. *'It has given me the greatest pleasure to see the boy grow up into a young man I can be proud of. His wife is a lovely girl, and I hope they will be very happy. I'm only sorry that I couldn't take Alicia to the church to see such a radiant bride, but, thank God, Eugénie chose not to come.'*

Contented as he was, Albert never forgot Poland and his desire to return. He followed the news avidly, and made sure that he was in touch with those in London who knew more than the papers reported. Every year he tried for visas for himself and John. 'I could never go back with father,' he told John, 'But surely you and I will make it. I so want you to see the country where grandfather and I were born, even if we can't get to Mieszki Wielkie.'

Then, at dawn on 14 August 1980, three days after Vicky had presented Albert with his first grandson, a previously sacked electrical fitter called Lech Walesa climbed into the Lenin shipyard in Gdansk to lead a strike over the illegal dismissal of a fellow-worker. He knew from bitter experience that workers out in the open were no match for tanks, and so he demanded that representatives of the government came to him in the shipyard to listen to his demands. This sparked off well planned, similar sit-ins throughout the country. The Party quickly assessed his strength and signed an agreement with the workers. A whole package was agreed, which included access to the media, civil rights and, even more staggering, the legal formation of free trade unions.

Thus 'Solidarity' was born. Soon it had over ten million members, which represented nearly everyone of working age. This time the Party had not only lost control, it was falling apart. Millions of its members handed in their cards and joined Solidarity. The scent of freedom was in the air, and the people were determined it would not be another false dawn. There was a new optimism on the streets, despite the ominous political situation and the catastrophic state of the economy. People saw Solidarity as a compromise between their democratic aspirations and their seemingly inescapable position within the Warsaw Pact.

There were, however, to be many more hurdles for the Polish people to climb. At first, the Soviet Union tolerated what was happening because it was unable to intervene, tied up as it was with the invasion of Afghanistan, and diplomatically isolated as a result, but it could not afford to see its apparat dismantled in Poland. The Party might be weak, but it still had the strength to crack the whip, and in February 1981, General Jaruzelski was appointed as Prime Minister. He was a man blindly faithful to Moscow, and immediately ordered a clamp-down, with thousands of people dragged from their beds on the night of 13 December and taken to prisons and concentration camps. Eventually, in 1982, Solidarity was dissolved in the courts. The Poles had always known however that the road to democracy would never be easy, and they were not in the mood to let it crumble back into dust.

1982, apart from the birth of his second grandson, also heralded the end of Albert's 'Peaceful Period', as he put it. The longed-for visas still didn't come, and by then he was growing a little desperate, suspecting that he was ill. *'I have pains which I can't explain, I feel sick at night, am beginning to lose weight and sleep badly. I have a growing feeling that I may have cancer. Alicia keeps telling me to go the doctor, but what's the point? If I have cancer, they can't cure me anyway.'*

For eighteen months he tried to lead a normal life, fighting against the pain and sickness. At times he was fine, and managed to enjoy the parties; at other times it was a struggle to get out of the house. Alicia did her best to bolster his morale and guide him as gently as possible towards the acceptance of a less hectic life. He proved a difficult patient, never prepared to admit that he was too ill to do something. In his diary he wrote, '*I feel so tired at times that all I want to do is sit down and cry. My darling Alicia looks on and tries to humour me, knowing there is little she can do, and John and she continuously advise me to go the doctor.*'

It was not until October 1983 that he walked into the surgery, and by that time it was too late. The doctors confirmed it was cancer of the liver and pancreas, and informed him he would be lucky to live a year. '*Although I suspected cancer, the blow is unbelievable,*' he wrote. '*I had expected many more years with Alicia and John. I feel the cold hand of fear gripping my stomach. The thought of more pain reduces me to a blubbering wreck. I must put a brave face on my suffering for Alicia's sake. Oh God, will I get back to Poland before I die?*'

The one person determined he should was John, and he now took up the regular telephone calls to the Embassy. As had happened before with his father, the noises were encouraging but that was all. Then, out of the blue on 24 May 1984, the visas were granted. It had taken twenty-eight years. '*What a wait!*' Albert wrote. '*Now that I can go, I fear I may be too ill to enjoy it. But if it is the last thing I do on earth, I'm going!*'

Alicia and John knew there was no time to waste and on 3 June, John and Albert flew to Warsaw.

'If he dies out there,' Alicia said to John the day before they left, 'Try and have him buried there, even if I can't get out. I'm sure that is what he would like.'

So much had changed in Warsaw that Albert hardly recognised it. '*It was a strange city to me. I tried to show John the State Bank from where we had set out with the gold bullion, but that had moved. Everything was different, and I felt lost in my own capital. It came as a blow that I felt so out of place. But thank God Kracow was different, hardly touched by the ravages of war. I was able to take him to what had been the cavalry school, showed him houses where we had flirted with beautiful well-bred girls, and many other places that I remembered with affection. Kracow did me good, and I felt much better after two weeks. So well, in fact, that I suggested we went to Budapest on the way home to see if I could find Helene's grave but, as usual, Communist bureaucracy stood in our way, and we had to abandon the idea. Pity really – I would have liked to have told her I would soon be joining her.*

'*Now I'm home again, I'm full of sadness. The pain has increased and I have nothing to look forward to, although my two grandsons are a constant joy to me. But I will never see Mieszki Wielkie again, and I will almost certainly be dead before I can go back to Poland to live. England has given me much, and I'm not ungrateful, but home will always be that large grey house tucked amongst the woods of eastern Poland. As I wait for death I long for the rose garden and the golden fish leaping at the flies in the evening twilight. I would like to take a last walk through the green forests, and hear the rustle of the boar in the undergrowth. In many ways, I'm dying an unhappy man, and yet I've had so much. Love, a son, grandchildren, excitement and many friends. Nevertheless, I believe I would exchange all that for just a week at Mieszki Wielkie. Perhaps, however, that is a dying man talking – I cannot be sure. My hand shakes and the pain eats into my system, I grow thin and bad-tempered. It is perhaps time to leave this world and go and join all those friends who died so that I could live in freedom, and taste all the things that they were so cruelly denied.'*

He died on 7 August 1984. The last entry in his diary, written two days before, reads: *'I feel I'm going soon. I'm terrified. Although the pain is at times unbearable, I have no desire to die. What will happen to me – oh God, it is frightening. But I suppose when the moment comes I will know nothing. What then? A dark unseeing hole, or my family greeting me? Ha, I have never believed in the after-life. But now . . . dear God, I'm hoping. When you read this, Alicia, ignore the rantings of a frightened man and just remember I love you. And John . . . try one day to return to our home.'*

Epilogue

Soon after Albert's death Alicia sold the house in Edinburgh and settled in their home in Chelsea where she still lives today. Aged 67, she is as striking and vivacious as ever, and pays regular visits to East Sheen Cemetery where Albert and his parents are buried.

Barbara and Kasimir continued to live in Scotland until his death in 1985 when she moved to Kent. Their two children are married and live in Canada.

John has only seen his sister Ewa once since his mother walked out on his father. She eventually qualified as a teacher and went to a British Military school in Germany where she met and married an Australian Major on secondment to the British army. She now lives in Australia.

John, Vicky, and the boys, Nicholas and Alexander, live outside Salisbury and John runs several businesses connected with pharmaceuticals. He has returned to Poland three times since his father's death: in 1987 on his own, in 1989 with Vicky and his two sons, and again in 1990, when he bought a small estate sixty kilometres from Kracow.

In spite of all the dramatic changes that have taken place since 1990, with the collapse of the Eastern Block and the break-up of the Soviet Union, John accepts that returning to live at Mieszki Wielkie can only be a dream, although for one woman of Russian descent this same dream became a reality in November 1992. Mrs Valya Schooling from Berwickshire, the only remaining direct descendant of the Korostovetzes, personal friends of the Tsar and one of Russia's most influential families before the revolution, was handed back the 6,000-acre estate Peresash near Chernigov by the Ukranian authorities which had been seized from the family seventy years before. It is questionable to say the least whether a descendent of a Polish aristocratic family will have the same good fortune.

Finally, what is Poland's future now? It is difficult to make a prediction, for democracy is still in its infancy, but given the strong vein of independence that has run through every generation, it seems hard not to believe that the newest generation won't grab their chance and make a success of it.

It was aided by what must have been one of the most emotional moments for the country in a long while when, on 28 October 1992, Poland saw the withdrawal of Soviet troops. Lech Walesa, by then the Polish president, declared, 'With the withdrawal of Russian troops from Czechoslavakia and Hungary already completed, Eastern Germany is now the only central European territory where ex-Soviet fighting forces remain. Few tears are being shed as the "glorious liberators" belatedly go home.'

Thus, almost half a century after sweeping into Poland to end the Nazi occupation and impose Communist rule, the last vestiges of the once great Red Army beat an ignominious retreat to an uncertain future in their mother country.

As one ordinary Pole was heard to remark, 'Historical justice is done. Poland, our beloved country that has suffered so much, is free at last.'